P9-AFV-574

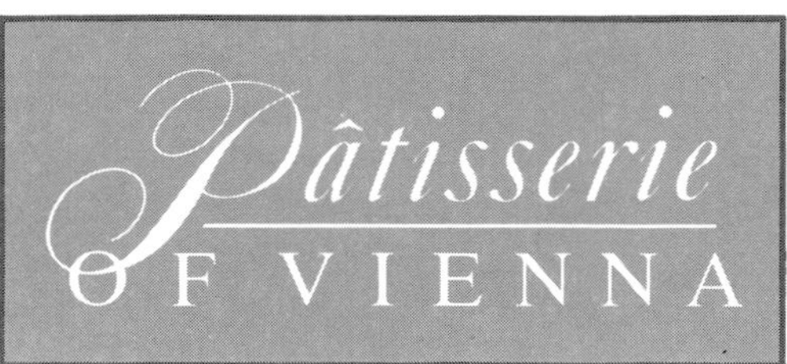
Pâtisserie
OF VIENNA

McGRAW-HILL BOOK COMPANY

New York St. Louis San Francisco
Hamburg Mexico

The author would particularly like to thank Mrs Lisl Ullmann, formerly of Vienna, now of Hampstead, London, for her valuable assistance. Thanks also to the 'guinea pigs' who tasted the recipes, namely Vanessa Vasey, Jonquil Phelan, Geoffrey Bond, David Lewis, Kate Evelyn Hackman and Hanna Bacon.

All eggs are large unless otherwise stated

First U.S. publication by McGraw-Hill Book Company in 1988

First published in Great Britain in 1988
by Macdonald & Co (Publishers) Ltd
London & Sydney

A member of BPCC plc

1 2 3 4 5 6 7 8 8 9 2 1 0 9 8

Library of Congress Cataloging-in-Publication Data

Bacon, Josephine, 1942-
Pâtisserie of Vienna.
"A Macdonald Orbis book"—Verso t.p.
1. Pastry–Austria–Vienna. 2. Cookery, Austrian.
I. Title
TX773.B23 1988 641.8'65 87-35386

ISBN 0-07-023317-9

Typeset by Tradespools, Frome

Printed and bound in Great Britain by
Purnell Book Production Limited
A member of BPCC plc

Editor: Gillian Prince
Text Editor: Norma MacMillan
Art Director: Bobbie Colegate-Stone
Designer: Frances de Rees
Photographer: Martin Brigdale
Stylist: Andrea Lambton
Home Economist: Maxine Clark

Introduction

Vienna, once the capital of an empire which stretched from Russia in the east to Naples in the south and included most of Eastern Europe, is renowned for good living, and especially its exquisite cakes and pastries. The Austrians have suffered the same hardships as all other Europeans. The Hungry Thirties were no less hungry for them than for anyone else, and the aftermath of World War II, including Russian occupation, was by no means a time of plenty. Yet these periods of austerity have left no trace on the Austrian diet, and the Viennese indulge in large meals and plenty of coffee and whipped cream, just as they did at the height of their prosperity during the Austro-Hungarian empire.

The Viennese still spend as much time as possible in cafés such as the famous Demel's, drinking their own special blend of coffee laced with ground fig seeds, and enjoying extravagant cakes laced with *Schlagobers*, or whipped cream. Indeed, Viennese café proprietors show little inclination to whisk the customer off the premises as soon as his or her cup and plate look empty; one can linger for hours over a modest *Mélange* (milky coffee), browsing through the newspapers and magazines thoughtfully provided by the establishment.

The coffee habit is so deeply ingrained in Vienna because the Viennese introduced this beverage into the western world. In 1683, while Vienna was being besieged by the Turks, a merchant named Kolschitzky, from a suburb of Vienna called Leopoldstadt, worked as an Austrian spy behind the Turkish lines. When victory was proclaimed and the siege lifted, Kolschitzky asked to be given the sacks of strange black beans that the Turks had left behind. The city fathers were happy to grant his request; if he could think of some use for them, then good luck to him!

Kolschitzky opened his coffee house which he called *zur blauen Flasche* (At the Sign of the Blue Bottle) and, dressed in Turkish garb, served this strange drink which he had learned to enjoy from the Turks. With a few refinements added – milk and sugar, for instance – it soon caught on. It was also felt appropriate to nibble on something while drinking. The plain roll which at first accompanied the drink soon blossomed into the elaborate creations found in today's coffee houses. One Turkish custom which has remained is the provision of a glass of water with the coffee. In hard times, the glasses of water have been more plentiful and have tasted better than the coffee!

The Viennese coffee house has been compared to a gentleman's club in England, and indeed ladies did not enter them until the nineteenth century. It was in the coffee houses that the Strausses, father and son, first played their waltzes; Schubert and his friends frequented the Café Bogner. It is doubtful whether some of the more extravagant examples of the pâtissier's art could have developed without the coffee house.

Yet the consumption of large quantities of cakes and pastries is not confined to the coffee house and restaurant. No one would consider entertaining a guest at home without providing some *Gugelhupf* to eat with the mandatory coffee, and one does not even need the excuse of visitors. The Viennese tend to eat cake as a dessert after meals – although they also have puddings on occasion.

Of course, cakes and pastries are an essential feature of the *Jause*, or coffee break, which is the Austrian equivalent of the British teatime. *Jause* can be enjoyed with one's friends in a café or at home.

No doubt the Viennese way of life has influenced the extent to which home baking is practiced, even today in the era of fast food. Housewives still devote themselves to providing the good things of life, using the excellent flour from the wheat and rye fields of Hungary and Romania, walnuts, almonds and hazelnuts from Carinthia, chestnuts from the south Tyrol, poppyseeds and plums from Hungary and Czechoslovakia, and the rich milk and cream from cows fed on mountain pastures in the Austrian alps.

All these conditions have helped to produce a cornucopia of cakes and pastries which has given Vienna its leading position in the art of pâtisserie.

SPECIAL EQUIPMENT AND INGREDIENTS

Some special baking equipment is shown on pages 10–11. You can decide for yourself what is essential and what is not. For example, the *Rehrücken* mold is not essential, as cakes can be baked in a loaf pan instead, but it makes the cakes look more attractive if you can get the right mold.

Ovens do not always heat to the exact temperature they register. If you suspect your oven is too hot or too cool, despite the fact that you have put it on the correct setting, it is a good idea to check it by using a separate oven thermometer.

There are a few unusual ingredients you will need for baking Viennese pâtisserie.

Vanilla sugar: Instead of using vanilla extract, Austrians put a vanilla bean in a tightly sealed container of sugar, so that the sugar is subtly permeated with the vanilla flavor. The vanilla bean needs to be added to the sugar at least 2 weeks before use. Vanilla sugar is also available in packets in many supermarkets.

Oblaten (wafers): These are large flat wafers a little like ordinary ice cream wafers but much bigger. They are available at gourmet food shops, but if you cannot find them, use ice cream wafers arranged in a circle, or several sheets of rice paper. Rice paper is available from good cookware shops.

Plum butter: This is sold under the name of *powidl* or *powidla* at gourmet food shops. It is imported from Poland or Czechoslovakia, and there is really no substitute. It is thick and smooth and has a slightly metallic taste. It is quite easy to find.

Sour salt (citric acid crystals): This is used very sparingly to give a strongly sour flavor. Buy it from special food sections of large supermarkets or kosher food stores.
Cake and graham cracker crumbs: A lot of Viennese cake recipes use leftover cake crumbs as an ingredient. If you don't have such a thing in your kitchen, use crushed graham crackers instead. Put them in a plastic bag and crush them with a rolling pin, or grind them in a food processor. (The latter method works best for cake crumbs.) Sift the crumbs afterwards to ensure there are no lumps left. Cake crumbs should be made from plain sponge cakes, such as the Basic Sponge Cake recipe (page 118).
Citron peel: Citrons make the finest candied peel. The peel is green in color and is often imported from Italy. However, it is expensive and hard to find. Instead, look for candied lemon and orange peel in health food stores and large supermarkets. Soak it in warm water for 20 minutes to make it easier to handle before chopping finely.
Chocolate: Always use the best quality baking chocolate you can find. It really makes an enormous difference to the final product.
Poppyseeds: Although whole poppyseeds are used in Austria for sprinkling on breads before baking, all the recipes in this book requiring poppyseeds use them ground. It is only when ground that they release their true flavor. Always use the black variety, not the white ones available from Indian food shops. It is most advisable to buy them from grocers specializing in central and eastern European foods, where the seeds may also be freshly ground in the shop. If you buy poppyseeds from supermarkets and ordinary grocers, they will come in very small quantities, be expensive, and may be stale.

BAKING HINTS

The recipes in this book range from childishly simple to fairly complicated. Emphasis has been placed above all on the ultimate taste of the cakes and pastries, rather than elaborate decoration. A cake split into six layers, and topped with piped icing, spun sugar and chocolate shapes and other handmade embellishments will taste no better than a two-layer iced cake with little decoration, if any. Better to leave the really complicated creations to the professional pastry-cooks with their expensive equipment and trained army of helpers.

Excellent results can be achieved with all the recipes, even the more complicated ones, if a few basic rules are followed.

Sponge Doughs without Baking Powder

Traditional Viennese baking used no leavening agents other than yeast and egg whites. Although a form of baking powder – ammonium carbonate, known as hartshorn – was used in Germany before the invention of modern baking powder, it was not popular in Austria. Baking powder is used much more frequently today, because it saves time and is almost foolproof, but it is only employed as a yeast substitute. The classic leavening agent is still stiffly beaten egg whites. The more stiffly they are beaten, the more air is incorporated into the cake.

The best way to beat egg whites is to use a copper bowl. The salts in the copper combine with the egg to make the whites stiff. Use a balloon whisk rather than a whisk in any other shape or a rotary beater, to incorporate more air. If you do not have a copper bowl, use an ordinary bowl and add a pinch of salt or cream of tartar to the whites. A countertop electric mixer also beats egg whites very well, but a food processor or blender are quite useless. Whites beat much better at room temperature.

Always ensure the egg whites are completely free of any yolk before beating. For safety's sake, when using the whites of more than one egg, separate each egg individually into two small bowls, before adding whites to the beating bowl, in case a yolk breaks in one egg.

Incorporate the whites into the main mixture with a cutting and folding motion, using a plastic or metal spatula or a large metal spoon. Put the cake into the oven as soon as possible after mixing, to ensure the whites remain firm.

To prevent the cake sinking after baking, allow it to cool inside the oven for least 30 minutes, with the heat turned off and the door ajar. If your kitchen is especially drafty, leave the cake for longer, or transfer it to a microwave oven with the door closed, to provide a draft-free atmosphere until the cake has reached room temperature. Refrigerate the cake until it is to be iced.

Rolled Cakes and Pastries

Many Viennese cakes, including strudel, are made of a dough rolled out, spread with filling and rolled up like a jelly roll. This rolling process can be tricky, but will be made easier if two important rules are observed. Firstly, always roll the dough out on a work surface on which you have first placed a cloth or a sheet of wax paper or nonstick parchment paper. The cloth or paper should be thickly sprinkled with flour. To roll the dough, lift the paper with the dough on it and flip the dough over. Secondly, always allow the filling to cool to room temperature before spreading it over the dough; if it is too hot, it will melt the dough.

Yeast Doughs

All your utensils and materials for yeast baking need to be warm, to encourage the yeast to grow. It is a good idea to rinse your mixing bowl in hot water and dry it quickly before use, and some people briefly warm the flour in a very cool oven. Dried yeast is more convenient than fresh, because of its keeping qualities, but fresh yeast is preferred by many people. If you are using dried yeast, always read the instructions carefully first. Some new varieties of yeast must not be mixed with liquid in the traditional way, but

Rehrücken mold, gugelhupf mold & springform pan

Bishop's Bread & Marble Cake

should be incorporated straight into the flour. If you are using one of these yeasts, adjust the recipe accordingly. If you are using a dried yeast which needs liquid, it is a good idea to combine it with the liquid (usually milk) and add a teaspoon of the sugar.

The yeast and liquid, and subsequently the yeast dough, should always be kept in a warm environment, so that the yeast can quickly start work on the dough. In winter, and in wet or cool weather, a gas oven with a pilot light or even an oven on its lowest setting is good. Alternatively, a microwave oven also provides a draft-free environment, similar to that of the large chests called dough-raisers that were once used for the purpose.

When combining the yeast liquid with the flour, the mixture must be kneaded for 5–10 minutes to reach the right consistency. This kneading releases the gluten, the elastic component, in the flour, on which the yeast feeds. The easiest way to knead a dough is using the dough hook on a heavy duty (countertop) electric mixer, although all the recipes in this book can also be made by hand.

To let the dough rise, it should be put into a clean very large bowl that has been lightly greased and covered either loosely with a damp cloth or with oiled plastic wrap. Make sure there is plenty of room for the dough to rise. A soft dough should double in bulk; this takes from 1½–2 hours, depending on atmospheric conditions and temperature. A firm dough may simply look "puffy" when ready. The test is to insert two fingers into the dough. If the dough does *not* spring back into shape, it is ready.

Most of the doughs described here need two risings. After the first rising, the dough is "punched down," i.e. beaten back into shape. At this stage it is usually shaped or put into the baking pan. It is then left to rise again. This takes much less time than the first rising, about 45 minutes to 1 hour. Again, the dough should be covered with a damp cloth or plastic wrap, to prevent it drying out.

If you do not want to bake a yeast dough immediately, there is no need to do so. Kneaded doughs can be covered and refrigerated in the least cold part of the refrigerator for at least 8 hours. This very slow rising can actually improve the quality of the crumb of the finished cake or bread, and is used extensively by professional bakers. However, the rising process is very slow and the dough cannot be baked for at least 6 hours; it must also be left in warm air for another hour for the yeast to start working quickly again.

Yeast doughs are usually baked at relatively high temperatures. However, very rich doughs, containing lots of eggs and fruit that might burn are often baked at lower temperatures than plain ones.

Pastrymaking

Just as all the ingredients and equipment for yeast doughs must be warmed, all the ingredients for pastrymaking should be as cold as possible. Food processors are excellent for pastrymaking, since pastry should touch the hands as little as possible, to keep it light. Generally, cold butter is cut into flour to make a mixture of bread crumb consistency, and just enough liquid is incorporated to make the crumbs stick together into a firm dough. The dough is then kneaded as briefly as possible. Rolling out must also be done quickly, as too much handling ruins the pastry.

Confusingly, all these rules are broken for Yeast Puff Dough (page 119), a strictly Viennese invention, but they are very important for all other types of pastry.

CONFECTIONERY AND SUGAR BOILING

Children love to help in the kitchen, and they can certainly be allowed to make uncooked cakes and confectionery. However, most sweets involve the making of a sugar syrup, and children should not be around when sugar is being boiled as it can be a dangerous substance. Not only does it have to be boiled at high temperatures for periods as long as 15 minutes, but if it spills it sticks firmly to whatever it has spilled on.

If you are going to make sugar syrups, a candy thermometer is an essential item of equipment because it takes all guesswork out of what can be a tricky operation. Professional confectioners even use a special measure called a Baumé gauge to test the density of syrup.

The stages of sugar boiling used in this book are:

Small thread or Short thread	217°F
Large thread or Long thread	230°F
Soft ball	240°F
Hard ball	250°F
Soft crack	270°F
Hard crack	300°F

Another essential piece of equipment is a heavy-based pan. The ideal sugar-boiling pans are made of untinned copper, but they are very expensive, so at least get a stainless steel one with a copper base. This will distribute the heat evenly and ensure the syrup does not burn. The length of time it must boil depends entirely on the quality of the pan: one which conducts heat poorly may make the syrup take ages to get to the right temperature. Always have a jug of hot water handy when boiling sugar, to dip the sugar thermometer in to warm it before use and rinse it afterwards.

Chocolate should always be melted at a low temperature. If it is allowed to heat too much it will lose its nice shiny glaze when set. Melt it in a bowl over simmering water or the top of a double boiler.

Hazelnut Jam Tart

LINZERTORTE

SERVES 8–10

2 sticks (8 oz) butter, softened
¾ cup all-purpose flour, sifted
½ cup granulated sugar
1¾ cups ground hazelnuts (filberts)
1 tsp ground cinnamon
½ tsp ground mace
½ tsp ground cloves
2 tbsp dark rum
2 tsp grated lemon zest
2 tsp grated orange zest
1 egg, separated
1 egg yolk
2 hard-cooked egg yolks
⅓ cup thick raspberry jam or plum butter
⅓ cup blueberry or blackberry jam
3 tbsp confectioners' sugar

Lightly grease a shallow 9 inch loose-bottomed cake pan or tart mold, preferably a nonstick one.

Beat the softened butter with the flour, granulated sugar, ground hazelnuts, spices, rum, lemon and orange zests, 2 raw egg yolks and the hard-cooked egg yolks. Make into a smooth, stiff dough. Cover the dough and refrigerate for 1 hour.

Roll out three-quarters of the dough and use it to line the bottom and 1 inch up the sides of the pan, pressing it well into the corners. Spread the raspberry jam or plum butter over the dough, then spread the blueberry or blackberry jam on top. Roll out the rest of the dough into an oblong about ¼ inch thick. Use a sharp knife or pastry wheel to cut the dough into ½ inch wide strips. Arrange the strips in a lattice pattern over the filling. Use any leftover dough to make a decorative border. Brush the dough with the lightly beaten egg white. Refrigerate the tart for 30 minutes.

Preheat the oven to 350°F. Bake the tart for 45 minutes or until it is lightly browned. Unmold it by standing the pan on a tall wide tin, such as a cookie tin. Sprinkle it with the sifted confectioners' sugar. Serve at room temperature. This tart will keep fresh for weeks if stored in an airtight tin.

Chestnut Gâteau

KASTANIENTORTE

Sweet chestnut trees grow in the Austrian lowland, especially around the lakes. You may find it more convenient to use canned unsweetened chestnut purée instead of dried chestnuts, in which case you will need 6 oz (about 3/4 cup), plus extra for the chestnut purée decoration, and you must beat the sugar into the canned purée before use. However, the flavor will not be quite as good.

SERVES 6

	To decorate
6 oz peeled dried chestnuts	scant ½ cup chestnut purée
2 cups milk	2 tbsp confectioners' sugar
2 inch piece vanilla bean	
2 tbsp granulated sugar	
3 eggs, separated	
1¼ cups confectioners' sugar	
1 cup cake crumbs	
⅔ cup heavy cream	
1 tbsp rum	

Soak the chestnuts in the milk with the vanilla bean overnight. When ready to make the cake, split the vanilla bean over the milk, so the tiny seeds fall into it; discard the bean. Pour the milk and chestnuts into a saucepan, add the granulated sugar and bring to a boil. Simmer, half-covered, for 20 minutes or until the chestnuts are soft.

Preheat the oven to 350°F. Line the bottom and sides of an 8 inch square cake pan with nonstick parchment paper.

Drain the chestnuts and purée them in a food processor. Whisk the egg yolks with half the sifted confectioners' sugar until pale yellow. In a separate bowl, beat the egg whites into stiff peaks. Fold half the chestnut purée and the cake crumbs into the egg yolk mixture, followed by the egg whites. Pour the mixture into the prepared pan and bake for 40 minutes, or until a toothpick inserted in the center comes out dry.

Unmold the cake on to a wire rack. Remove the lining paper and let the cake cool completely before slicing it into 2 equal layers.

Whip the cream with the rest of the sifted confectioners' sugar, and add the rum while whipping. Fold in the rest of the chestnut purée. Use half the mixture to sandwich the cake layers together, and pile the remainder on the top. Smooth with a palette knife to make an even layer.

To decorate, pipe more chestnut purée on the top of the cake, and dredge with the confectioners' sugar.

Strawberry Shortcake

ERDBEERTORTE

This is the original Strawberry Shortcake that is now so popular in the United States. In fact, many American cakes and pastries originated in German-speaking countries.

SERVES 10

1½ sticks (6 oz) butter, softened
¾ cup all-purpose flour, sifted
¾ cup sugar
¾ cup ground almonds
grated zest and juice of 1 lemon
1 egg white, lightly beaten
1½ lb ripe strawberries (about 5 cups)
2 envelopes unflavored gelatin
1 cup + 2 tbsp water
a few drops of red food coloring
whipped cream, to decorate

Preheat the oven to 300°F.

Combine the butter, flour, half of the sugar, the ground almonds and lemon zest into a stiff dough, ideally using a food processor. Roll it out on a floured board until it is about ⅛ inch thick. Slide the dough on to a buttered and floured baking sheet, trimming it to fit. Use the trimmings to make a rim around the edge, attaching it securely by dampening the dough. Brush all over with the egg white. Bake for 20 minutes; do not let the pastry brown.

Let the pastry cool to room temperature, then arrange the most attractive of the strawberries over it; you should have about a third of the strawberries left over.

Soften the gelatin in ½ cup water. Purée the remaining strawberries, then put them into a saucepan with the remaining water, the lemon juice, the rest of the sugar, and the food coloring. Cook, stirring, until the mixture thickens slightly. Remove the pan from the heat and stir in the softened gelatin until it has dissolved. Pour the mixture over the strawberries, then leave to cool and set. Serve decorated with whipped cream.

Illustrated on page 19

Cheesecake & Strawberry Shortcake

Apple Cake

APFELTORTE

Any kind of jam can be used, but ginger-flavored jam or plum butter (powidl) makes this cake especially delicious. Sieve the jam before using if it contains large pieces of fruit.

SERVES 8

2 sticks (8 oz) butter
1⅔ cups all-purpose flour, sifted
⅔ cup sugar
1 egg, separated
grated zest and juice of 1 lemon
2 tbsp ground almonds
1½ lb tart crisp apples
¼ cup water
2 tbsp jam
1 tbsp raisins

Preheat the oven to 325°F. Butter a 10 inch tart or quiche mold.

Work the butter and flour together with a pastry blender or two knives, or in a food processor, until the mixture resembles bread crumbs. Add 6 tbsp of the sugar, the egg yolk, grated lemon zest and ground almonds. Knead the dough just until it is smooth, then wrap and leave it in a cool place to rest and firm up for at least 30 minutes.

Roll out about two-thirds of the dough until it is about ¼ inch thick. Use it to line the tart mold, pressing it over the bottom and up the sides. Reserve the dough trimmings. Line the pastry case with foil, sprinkle uncooked rice into it and bake unfilled for 20 minutes; discard the foil and rice after baking.

Meanwhile, make the filling. Peel, quarter and core the apples, and sprinkle with the lemon juice. Put them into a heavy saucepan with the rest of the sugar and the water and cook until soft, stirring to make a purée. Add the jam and raisins. Allow to cool slightly, then pour the mixture into the pastry case.

Roll out the remaining dough and trimmings to ¼ inch thick. Use a sharp knife or a pastry wheel to cut long ½ inch wide strips. Arrange the strips of dough in a lattice pattern over the filling: seal the dough strips to the rim with a little water. Roll the rest of the dough into a sausage shape and arrange this around the rim of the mold, pressing it into a decorative pattern. Brush the dough with lightly beaten egg white. Bake for 30 minutes, or until the pastry is golden brown.

Instead of topping the cake with a lattice of dough, it can be topped with meringue, in which case it becomes known in Austria as Swedish Apple Cake. Bake with the meringue topping only until it is starting to color, about 15 minutes.

Poppyseed Sponge Cake

MOHNTORTE

Poppyseeds are a favorite ingredient for all kinds of cakes and breads in Austria. Please read the note on page 8 before making this cake.

SERVES 8

6 tbsp unsalted butter, softened
¾ cup granulated sugar
4 eggs, separated
about 1 cup poppyseeds, freshly ground
2 tbsp chopped mixed candied peel
grated zest of 1 lemon
1 tbsp rum
6 tbsp confectioners' sugar

Preheat the oven to 325°F. Butter and flour an 8 inch loose-bottomed cake pan.

Beat the butter and granulated sugar together until creamy, then beat in the egg yolks. Add the poppyseeds, chopped peel, lemon zest and rum. Beat the egg whites into stiff peaks and fold them into the mixture.

Pour the mixture into the pan, and bake for 1 hour or until a toothpick inserted in the center comes out dry. Leave the cake in the turned-off oven for another hour, with the door ajar, so that it cools slowly. Unmold it and dredge it with the sifted confectioners' sugar. Cool it on its base on a wire rack. Refrigerate the cake until required.

Hungarian Dobos Cake

DOBOSTORTE

SERVES 12

	Filling
4 extra large eggs	**12 oz semisweet chocolate**
1½ cups granulated sugar	**1½ sticks (6 oz) unsalted butter, softened**
2 tbsp vanilla sugar	**3 cups confectioners' sugar, sifted**
1 cup all-purpose flour	**3 egg yolks**
¾ cup chocolate sprinkles or toasted chopped nuts	
1 cup heavy cream	
8 shelled hazelnuts (filberts)	

Preheat the oven to 375°F. Line 3 baking sheets with nonstick parchment paper. Draw two 8 inch circles, using a plate or cake pan as a template, on each sheet of parchment paper. Butter and flour inside the circles and shake off the excess flour.

Whisk the eggs, ⅔ cup granulated sugar and the vanilla sugar together in the top of a double boiler or in a bowl over simmering water until the mixture is thick and foaming and doubled in bulk: it should leave a trail on itself when the whisk is lifted. Remove the bowl from the pan and continue whisking the mixture as it cools. Fold the sifted flour into the cooled egg mixture a little at a time. Divide this sponge batter between the baking sheets, spreading it evenly over the 6 marked circles.

Bake the sponge layers, in batches, for 8–10 minutes or until set and golden. Leave them to cool on the baking sheets for 5 minutes, then transfer them to wire racks to cool completely. Trim the layers, if necessary, making sure they are perfectly round and all the same size. Select the best one for the top of the cake and set aside.

Now make the topping. Place the cake layer to be used for the top on a greased wire rack. Melt the remaining granulated sugar in a heavy-based saucepan and bring it to a boil slowly, without stirring. Let it boil until it reaches the hard crack stage and turns golden-brown, but do not let it darken too much or it will be bitter. Have an oiled palette knife ready. Pour the caramel over the top sponge layer and spread it quickly with the palette knife before it cools. Cut the top into 8 equal sections with a sharp oiled knife before the caramel sets.

To make the filling, break the chocolate into a bowl placed over simmering water, or into the top of a double boiler. While the chocolate is melting, beat the softened butter with the confectioners' sugar using a wooden spoon until the mixture is light and fluffy. Beat in the egg yolks and then the melted chocolate. If the filling is too runny, chill it in the refrigerator for a few minutes.

Spread about half the filling on the remaining 5 cake layers. Arrange the layers on top of each other, and spread the rest of the filling over the sides and top of the cake. Use a palette knife to press the chocolate sprinkles or nuts against the side of the cake. Whip the cream until stiff and pipe 8 scrolls from the center to the outside of the cake. Lay the caramel triangles on top, "windmill" fashion. Use the remaining cream to pipe a rosette on top of each triangle, and decorate each with a hazelnut.

Saddle of Venison Cake

REHRÜCKEN

This cake is baked in the special rehrücken mold, although a 1½ quart capacity loaf pan will do. It is decorated with almonds to simulate the strips of pork fat used to lard roast venison.

SERVES 10

	Icing
⅔ cup fine graham cracker crumbs	¾ cup heavy cream
7 eggs, 5 separated	6 tbsp butter
¼ cup vanilla sugar	1 cup cocoa powder
1 tsp ground cinnamon	1 cup granulated sugar
3 tbsp finely chopped candied citron peel	¼ cup vanilla sugar
¾ cup ground almonds	1 cup blanched almonds, halved
3 oz semisweet chocolate, grated	
¼ cup granulated sugar	

Preheat the oven to 350°F. Liberally butter the mold or pan and sprinkle it with the graham cracker crumbs, shaking out the excess.

Beat the 5 egg yolks with the 2 whole eggs and the vanilla sugar until the mixture is thick and pale-colored. Beat in the cinnamon, citron peel, ground almonds and grated chocolate.

In another bowl, beat the 5 egg whites into stiff peaks, then gradually beat in the granulated sugar until the mixture forms stiff peaks again. Fold the egg white mixture into the chocolate mixture, cutting and folding with a plastic spatula until the mixture is homogenous, but do not mix too much.

Pour the batter into the prepared mold. Bake for 30 minutes, or until the cake has shrunk slightly from the sides of the mold. Turn off the oven and leave the cake inside, with the door ajar, to cool gradually for 1 hour, then unmold it on to a wire rack. Let it cool completely before icing it.

To make the icing, combine the cream, butter, cocoa, granulated sugar and vanilla sugar in a heavy-based saucepan. Cook the mixture over very low heat, stirring constantly, for about 5 minutes or until it is smooth and thick. Remove it from the heat and let it cool for about 5 minutes, then pour it over the cake evenly.

Stick the almonds upright into the cake, spaced regularly about 1 inch apart. Leave the cake to cool completely before serving, and slice it so that each portion contains a few almonds.

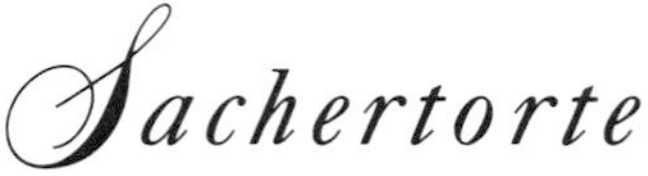

SACHERTORTE

Vienna's greatest cake, the creation of Franz Sacher, chef pâtissier to Prince Metternich, was once the subject of a seven-year lawsuit against a rival claiming equal authenticity. This is almost certainly why it is traditional to pipe the name "Sacher" on top of the cake, so you know you are eating the real thing.

SERVES 10

7 oz semisweet chocolate	***Chocolate icing***
1 stick butter	**3 oz semisweet chocolate**
8 eggs, separated	**1 cup heavy cream**
2 tsp vanilla sugar	**1 cup granulated sugar**
2 egg whites	**2 tbsp vanilla sugar**
pinch of salt	**1 tsp light corn syrup**
¾ cup granulated sugar	**1 egg**
¾ cup all-purpose flour	
⅔ cup apricot jam	

Preheat the oven to 350°F. Butter two 9 inch layer cake pans and line the bottoms with circles of nonstick parchment paper. Butter and flour the circles, and shake off the excess flour.

To make the sponge, break the chocolate into the top of a double boiler and heat it over simmering water until the chocolate melts, stirring occasionally. Melt the butter and pour it into a bowl. Add the egg yolks and vanilla sugar and stir well. Beat the chocolate into the mixture until it is smooth.

Beat the 10 egg whites with the salt until they form stiff peaks, then gradually beat in the granulated sugar. Fold the egg whites into the chocolate mixture. Sift the flour on top and fold in gently but thoroughly.

Pour the batter into the prepared pans, dividing it evenly. Bake for 30 minutes, or until the layers are dry and a toothpick inserted in the center comes out clean. Remove them from the oven and loosen the sides. Cool the cakes, still in the pans, on wire racks. When the cakes are cooled, unmold them.

To make the icing, break the chocolate into a heavy-based saucepan and add the cream, granulated sugar, vanilla sugar and corn syrup. Cook over low heat, stirring constantly with a wooden spoon, until the chocolate has melted, then stop stirring and raise the heat. Let the mixture boil for 5 minutes.

Beat the egg lightly in a mixing bowl, and stir 3 tbsp of the chocolate icing mixture into it. Pour this into the mixture in the saucepan and stir well to incorporate. Cook, stirring constantly, over low heat until the mixture coats the back of a spoon thickly; do not boil. Remove the pan from the heat and leave to cool.

Warm the jam until it has melted, then press it through a sieve. Spread one cake layer with the jam and put the other layer on top. Spread jam over the sides of the cake. Pour the icing over the cake and quickly smooth it with a palette knife. Refrigerate the cake for at least 2 hours.

Illustrated on page 26

Sachertorte & Schneider's Chocolate Cake

Schneider's Chocolate Cake

SCHNEIDERTORTE

Schneider was the owner of a popular nineteenth-century Viennese restaurant. This is his contribution to the best chocolate cake contest started by Sacher and Demel. If you cannot find ground walnuts and hazelnuts, buy them whole and grind them together in a coffee or nut grinder or blender.

SERVES 10

4 tbsp butter, softened	***Chocolate cream***
6 tbsp sugar	**6 tbsp sugar**
2 oz semisweet chocolate	**3 eggs**
6 eggs, separated	**1 tsp vanilla extract**
1¾ cups ground almonds	**1 tsp cornstarch**
1 quantity Chocolate Icing (page 120)	**2 oz semisweet chocolate**
	6 tbsp butter, softened
Little melted semisweet chocolate, to decorate (optional)	**½ cup ground walnuts**
	⅔ cup ground hazelnuts (filberts)

Preheat the oven to 325°F. Butter and flour a deep 9 inch cake pan.

Beat the butter and sugar together until light and fluffy. Melt the chocolate and add it with the egg yolks. Beat in the ground almonds. Beat the egg whites into stiff peaks and fold them into the mixture.

Pour the batter into the prepared pan, and bake for 50 minutes or until a toothpick inserted in the center comes out dry. Leave the cake to cool in the pan, then unmold it on to a wire rack. When it is cold, carefully slice it into three layers.

To make the chocolate cream, put the sugar, eggs, vanilla and cornstarch into the top of a double boiler and beat over simmering water until the mixture is thick. Leave to cool. Melt the chocolate and beat it with the butter until the mixture is smooth. Combine it with the mixture in the double boiler and beat in the ground nuts.

Use the chocolate cream to sandwich together the cake layers; if any is left over, spread it over the sides. Coat the top and sides of the cake with the chocolate icing. If liked, decorate the top with lines of piped melted semisweet chocolate.

Illustrated on page 27

Maytime Strawberry Cream Cake

MAICREMETORTE

If you cannot get wild strawberries, cut fresh ones into small pieces to simulate wild ones, or use raspberries or any soft fruit instead.

SERVES 10

2 egg yolks	*Strawberry cream*
4 eggs	½ lb strawberries (about 1½ cups)
grated zest of 1 lemon	1¼ cups heavy cream
⅔ cup sugar	¼ cup confectioners' sugar
6 tbsp butter, melted	1 tbsp wild strawberry liqueur or port wine
¾ cup all-purpose flour, sifted	*To decorate*
	¼ lb (about 1 cup) wild strawberries
	lilies-of-the-valley, white freesias or other spring flowers

Preheat the oven to 300°F. Butter and flour a deep 8 inch cake pan.

Put the egg yolks, whole eggs, lemon zest and sugar into the top of a double boiler and beat over simmering water until the mixture is thick. Sprinkle with the cooled melted butter and flour, and beat them in until the mixture is smooth.

Pour the mixture into the prepared cake pan, and bake for 30 minutes or until a toothpick inserted in the cake comes out clean. Leave to cool completely in the pan, then unmold the cake onto a wire rack.

To make the strawberry cream, hull the strawberries and purée them in a blender or food processor. Whip the cream until it stiffens, then fold it into the strawberry purée with the sifted confectioners' sugar. Beat in the liqueur or port wine.

Spread the strawberry cream thickly over the top and sides of the cake, and decorate with wild strawberries and fresh flowers.

Illustrated on pages 30–31

Maytime Strawberry Cream Cake

Viennese Meringue Cake

BAISERTORTE

This meringue basket can be made months in advance and stored in an airtight tin with plenty of confectioners' sugar to keep it dry. It is a good idea to bake the bottom of the cake separately on a sheet of edible rice paper, which does not need to be removed; this may avoid a heart-breaking accident! The best liqueurs to use are Kirsch, Strega or wild strawberry liqueur.

SERVES 10

	Filling
10 egg whites	**2½ cups heavy cream, chilled**
⅛ tsp cream of tartar	**¼ cup confectioners' sugar**
4 cups superfine sugar	**2 tbsp liqueur**
	1 lb strawberries, raspberries or blueberries (3–4 cups), hulled, washed and patted dry

Preheat the oven to 225°F.

Take 3 sheets of nonstick parchment paper, and use an 8 inch plate or baking pan to trace 2 circles on each sheet. Put one sheet of paper on a baking sheet.

Beat 8 of the egg whites with half the cream of tartar until they form soft peaks, then gradually beat in half of the superfine sugar. Continue beating until the mixture forms stiff peaks. Fold in ½ cup more of the sugar with a spatula.

Pile the mixture into a pastry bag fitted with a plain tube. Pipe a ring of meringue inside the edge of one of the drawn circles, on the paper on the baking sheet, and continue piping in an even spiral until you reach the center. Smooth over the spirals lightly with a rubber spatula, adding a little more meringue if there are any gaps between the rings of the spiral, as this will be the base of the cake. Pipe a ring of meringue inside the edge of the other circle on the same sheet of paper. Then pipe parallel diagonal lines in opposite directions to make a lattice pattern; this will be the lid.

Dry out the circles in the oven for 45 minutes. Remove them from the oven and carefully transfer, on their baking paper, to wire racks. Leave to cool.

Beat the remaining 2 egg whites with the rest of the cream of tartar until they form soft peaks, then gradually beat in the rest of the sugar and continue beating until stiff. Lay the remaining sheets of parchment paper on 2 baking sheets. Use some of the meringue mixture to pipe a single ring inside each of the 4 circles; refrigerate the remaining meringue until required. Dry out the meringue rings in the oven for 45 minutes, then transfer them, on the paper, to wire racks to cool.

When cold, carefully peel the meringue base from its paper and set it on an ovenproof serving dish. Peel each of the meringue rings from their paper and place them on top of each other on the base. Beat the reserved meringue, which will have gone a little soggy, and use it to "cement" together the meringue rings and to smooth over the sides of the meringue cake to hide the rings. If there is any meringue left over, put it into a pastry bag with a star tube and use it to pipe a decorative edge around the lattice lid. Return the cake and lid separately to the oven to dry for a final 20 minutes. Remove, cool and reserve until required.

When you are ready to serve the cake, whip the cream with the sifted confectioners' sugar and liqueur until it is stiff. Fold in the berries and pile the mixture into the cake. Set the lattice lid on top, slightly askew so that the berry mixture inside can be seen.

If preferred, the lattice lid may be omitted, and the top of the cake decorated with chocolate-dipped berries. Alternatively, use any seasonal fresh fruit instead of the berries and decorate the filled basket with frosted grapes.

Illustrated on pages 34–5

Viennese Meringue Cake

Cheesecake

TOPFENKUCHEN

There are almost as many recipes for cheesecake as there are Austrian bakers. This one is feather-light and is not too rich. It is not often realized that cheesecake does not have to be made with high-fat cheese and sour cream. Covering the bottom of the springform pan with foil before baking will ensure you can remove the cake easily from the base, and the shiny foil will help reflect the heat so the base does not cook too fast and become hard.

SERVES 10

	Filling
6 tbsp butter	6 eggs, separated
4 cups fine cake crumbs	1 cup sugar
1 tbsp ground cinnamon	grated zest and juice of 1 lemon
confectioners' sugar, fresh fruit (such as cherries and raspberries) or Crumb topping (see Yeast Crumb Cake, page 65), to decorate	¼ tsp sour salt (page 8)
	1 lb medium-fat or low-fat cream or pot cheese
	1 cup low-fat unflavored firm yogurt
	2 tbsp all-purpose flour
	1 tbsp rum (optional)

Preheat the oven to 350°F. Cover the bottom of a 9 inch springform pan neatly with foil, shiny side outward. Grease the bottom and side of the pan and leave them separate.

Melt the butter over low heat, then combine it with the crumbs. Add the cinnamon and stir. Pat most of the mixture on to the bottom of the pan, using the back of a spoon to make an even layer. Press the rest on to the side of the pan. Refrigerate both parts until required.

Beat the egg yolks with the sugar until smooth and fluffy. Beat in the lemon zest and juice, sour salt, cheese, yogurt, flour and rum. Beat the egg whites into stiff peaks and fold them into the mixture until the ingredients are well combined.

Assemble the springform pan and pour the cheese mixture into it. Sprinkle with the crumb topping, if used. Bake for 1 hour, then turn off the heat. Leave the cake to cool in the oven for at least another hour before removing. Loosen the side of the pan, but do not unmold the cake until you are ready to serve it. Refrigerate the cake when it has cooled completely. Before serving, dust with sifted confectioners' sugar and decorate with fresh fruit.

Illustrated on page 18

Coffee Nut Cake

NUSSTORTE MIT GRILLAGECREME

SERVES 8

6 tbsp sugar	***To decorate***
6 eggs, separated	**6 unblanched almonds**
¾ cup ground almonds	**6 walnut halves**
¾ cup ground walnuts	
1 cup cake crumbs	
1 quantity Coffee Praline Cream (page 125)	
1 quantity Coffee Icing (page 120)	

Preheat the oven to 325°F. Butter and flour a deep 9 inch cake pan.

Beat the sugar and egg yolks together until light and fluffy. Add the ground nuts; sift the crumbs and beat them into the mixture. Beat the egg whites into stiff peaks and fold them into the mixture.

Pour the mixture into the prepared pan, and bake for 40 minutes or until a toothpick inserted in the center comes out dry. Leave the cake to cool in the pan, then unmold it on to a wire rack. When it is cold carefully slice it into two layers.

Sandwich the cake layers together with some of the coffee praline cream, and use the rest to coat the sides. Spread the top with the coffee icing. Score the icing into 12 sections before it sets and decorate each with an unblanched almond or walnut half.

Rum Punch Cake

PUNSCHTORTE

If you want to cheat with this Austrian version of Tipsy Cake you can cut up two purchased sponge cakes, and heat the rum with 1 cup light corn syrup to make the rum punch syrup. Substitute grenadine for the rum in the syrup and omit alcohol from the icing for children.

SERVES 12

8 eggs, separated	***Rum punch syrup***
1¼ cups sugar	**4 sugar cubes**
¾ cup all-purpose flour, sifted	**2 lemons**
3 tbsp raspberry jam	**1 orange**
1 quantity Rum Punch Icing (page 121), tinted pink	**1 cup sugar**
	½ cup water
	¼ cup dark rum
	3 drops of pink or red food coloring
	3 drops of orange or yellow food coloring, or 1 tsp cocoa powder

Preheat the oven to 350°F. Butter and flour two 8 inch cake pans.

Beat the egg yolks with 1 cup of the sugar until the mixture is light and fluffy. Beat in the flour. Beat the egg whites until stiff with the rest of the sugar, and fold them into the mixture.

Pour the batter into the pans, dividing it equally, and bake for 30 minutes or until a toothpick inserted in the center comes out dry. Unmold from the pans and cool on wire racks.

Split one of the cakes into two layers. Spread the bottom layer with the jam and reserve it. Take the second cake and cut out the center right through to the base, leaving a 2 inch wide ring. Cut the center part that has been removed into small cubes.

To make the syrup, rub the sugar cubes over the lemons and orange, to flavor the sugar; reserve it. Squeeze the juice from the lemons and orange. Dissolve the sugar cubes and sugar in the water, then boil for 15 minutes to the large thread stage. Stir in the lemon and orange juices and the rum and bring back to a boil. Remove from the heat immediately, and divide the syrup between two bowls. Add the pink coloring to one bowl and the orange coloring or cocoa to the other. Divide the sponge cubes into three portions: soak one third in the pink syrup, one third in the orange, and leave the rest unsoaked.

Place the jam-covered layer of the cake on the base of a springform pan. Place the second cake ring over the jam-covered layer of cake. Pile the three portions of sponge cake cubes back into the center of the cake and top it with the plain layer of cake. Place the sides around the base of the springform pan, and put a double layer of wax or nonstick parchment paper over the top of the cake. Place another cake pan base over the top and weigh it down with two cans of food. Leave the cake for at least 8 hours in the refrigerator.

The next day, ice it with the punch icing. If liked, decorate with sugared flowers.

Family Cake

HAUSFREUNDE

This is the plain (by Austrian standards!) cake that Austrians keep in reserve for the unexpected guest, or for any other occasion when there is a desperate and sudden need for cake.

SERVES 8

¾ cup sugar
3 eggs, separated
1⅔ cups all-purpose flour, sifted
1¼ cups sliced almonds
1 cup raisins, sprinkled with 1 tsp flour

Preheat the oven to 325°F. Butter and flour a 1½ quart capacity loaf pan.

Beat the sugar and egg yolks together until light and fluffy. Beat in the flour, then stir in the almonds and raisins. Beat the egg whites into stiff peaks and fold them into the mixture.

Pour the batter into the loaf pan and bake for 30 minutes or until a toothpick inserted in the center comes out clean. Unmold the cake and cool on a wire rack.

To use the cake when cold, cut it into thin slices. Arrange the slices on baking sheets and put them into an oven on the lowest setting, or a gas oven with the pilot light lit. Leave for 30 minutes or until the slices have dried out and are lightly browned. These crisp slices are stored in an airtight tin with plenty of confectioners' sugar, and are served with coffee or with desserts.

Lightning Cherry Cake

BLITZKUCHEN MIT KIRSCHEN

This is another supposedly plain cake, this time filled with glacé cherries and candied peel; you can make it absolutely plain by omitting the cherries. It can be flavored with almond extract or vanilla extract instead of lemon.

SERVES 8

1 stick butter	***To decorate***
5 eggs, separated	**1 quantity Boiled Icing (page 120) flavored with Maraschino or Amaretto liqueur**
1½ cups sugar	**strips of candied angelica**
grated zest and juice of 1 lemon	**glacé cherries**
3 drops of lemon extract	
1⅓ cups all-purpose flour, sifted	
½ lb glacé cherries (about 1½ cups), tossed in flour	
⅓ cup chopped candied peel	

Preheat the oven to 350°F. Butter and flour an 8 inch cake pan.

Beat the butter until it is creamy, then beat in the egg yolks, sugar, lemon zest and juice and lemon extract. Beat in the flour. Beat the egg whites into stiff peaks and fold them into the mixture.

Pour half the mixture into the cake pan. Sprinkle it with the floured glacé cherries and candied peel, then pour the rest of the mixture over it. Bake for 45 minutes or until a toothpick inserted into the center comes out clean. Leave to cool in the turned-off oven, with the door ajar, for 1 hour, then unmold and cool completely on a wire rack.

Ice with white boiled icing and decorate with angelica and glacé cherries.

This cake can also be baked, without the cherries and candied peel, in a ring or savarin mold.

STRUDEL

There is a bitter argument between the Austrians and the Hungarians as to whether strudel or the Hungarian retes is the more delicious and the more traditional. Both are borrowed from their old enemies, the Turks, who invented this type of paper-thin dough. Continental grocers sell frozen strudelblätter (strudel leaves), but it is more satisfying to make the whole strudel from scratch.

MAKES ONE 18 inch OR TWO 9 inch STRUDELS (SERVES 18)

1⅔ cups all-purpose flour
1 egg yolk
¼ tsp salt
½ tsp flavorless oil
¼ cup lukewarm water
½ tsp white vinegar
all-purpose flour for sprinkling
2 sticks (8 oz) butter, melted
1 quantity Strudel Filling (pages 122–3)
6 tbsp confectioners' sugar

Sift the flour on to a work surface and make a well in the center. Put the egg yolk, salt, oil, water and vinegar into the well. Quickly mix to a dough with a knife (or put the ingredients in a food processor and blend them with the metal blade). When the dough coheres into a ball, knead it by hand on a floured board until it becomes elastic and does not stick to the board or your hands, about 10 minutes. Place it in a warmed bowl, cover and leave it in a warm place to rest for 45 minutes.

Cover a large table with a tablecloth or sheet, and sprinkle it liberally with flour. Put the dough on this surface and roll it out until it is about ¼ inch thick. Sprinkle the dough with flour and brush it well with about 4 tbsp of the melted butter. Put your hands, palms upward, underneath the dough and pull and stretch it out all around until it is stretched to the limit without breaking; it should be almost transparent (Austrians say you should be able to read a newspaper through it!). Cut off the thick edges with sharp scissors.

Preheat the oven to 450°F. Sprinkle a baking sheet (or 2, if your strudel looks like it is too long to fit on to one baking sheet) with water. Brush the dough all over with more melted butter. Spread the chosen filling over two-thirds of the dough nearest to you, to within ½ inch of the edge and leaving one-third of the dough bare. Roll the strudel up, starting at the filled end, by raising the tablecloth or sheet and letting the dough roll itself over and over. Fold the ends and seam underneath.

Cut the strudel in half if it is to fit on to 2 baking sheets. Slide the strudel or strudels on to the baking sheet or sheets and brush with the rest of the melted butter. Bake for 45 minutes or until brown and crisp. Dredge liberally with sifted confectioners' sugar, and slide on to wire racks to cool. Store in airtight tins.

Strudel with Cherry Filling

Austrian Jam Roll

BISKUITROLLE

This rolled-up cake is very popular in Vienna. The difference in flavor between the homemade variety and the purchased version is indescribable.

SERVES 8

6 eggs, separated
¾ cup sugar
1¾ cups all-purpose flour
4 tbsp butter, melted and cooled
¼ cup coarse sugar crystals or broken-up rock candy
⅔ cup raspberry or plum jam, warmed

Preheat the oven to 350°F. Thoroughly grease an 8 × 10 inch jelly roll pan and line it with nonstick parchment paper.

Beat the egg yolks with the sugar until light and fluffy. Beat in the flour. Whisk the egg whites into stiff peaks and fold them into the mixture. Sprinkle with the butter.

Spread the batter evenly in the pan, and bake for 30 minutes or until the cake is set firmly and comes away easily from the paper.

Lay a clean cloth on a work surface and sprinkle it with the sugar crystals. Unmold the cake onto the cloth and peel away the lining paper. Spread the warmed jam over the roll and roll it up quickly, starting at a short end. Transfer the rolled cake to a serving dish, seam downwards.

Almond or Hazelnut Ring Cake

NUSSTORTE

The berry garnish for this cake can be varied according to season; strawberries go best with almonds, and raspberries with hazelnuts. If you find whipped cream too rich, you can substitute a whipped mixture of half yogurt, half pot cheese. Or try one of the new subtly-flavored yogurts.

SERVES 12–14

½ cup fine graham cracker crumbs	***To finish***
2 cups sugar	**1½ cups heavy cream**
1 tsp ground allspice	**¼ cup confectioners' sugar**
1 tsp ground cinnamon	**3 tbsp Kirsch or other liqueur**
4 cups ground almonds or hazelnuts (filberts)	**1 lb strawberries or raspberries (3–4 cups), hulled**
grated zest of 1 lemon	
6 eggs, separated	
2 tsp salt	
1 tbsp light corn syrup	
2 tbsp water	
1 egg white, lightly beaten	

Preheat the oven to 350°F. Grease a 9 inch ring mold, and sprinkle it with the graham cracker crumbs.

Combine the sugar, spices, ground nuts and lemon zest. Beat the egg yolks until they are light and fluffy, then beat them into the nut mixture. Beat the egg whites with the salt into stiff peaks, and fold them gently but thoroughly into the nut mixture.

Spoon the mixture into the ring mold, bake for 40 minutes. Remove from the oven but do not turn the oven off. Leave the cake to cool in the mold for 5 minutes before loosening the sides with a palette knife. Invert the cake on to a wire rack, then transfer it to a baking sheet.

Mix the corn syrup with the water and brush this glaze over the cake. Brush it with the lightly beaten egg white, and return it to the oven to dry for 5 minutes. Remove and cool completely on a wire rack before transferring to a serving dish.

To make the fruit filling, whip the cream with the sifted confectioners' sugar until stiff, then beat in the Kirsch or other liqueur. Fold in the berries. Pile into the center of the cake.

Rich Chocolate Cake

HABSBURGERTORTE ODER KANZLERTORTE

As you can see, the German name for this cake is either, "Habsburg Cake" or "Prime Minister's Cake," depending on how up-to-date you want to be. Obviously, only the best was good enough for the highest in the land, and naturally enough that had to be chocolate.

SERVES 10

5 oz semisweet chocolate, broken into pieces	*Filling*
6 eggs, separated	5 oz semisweet chocolate
2 tbsp vanilla sugar	1¼ sticks (5 oz) unsalted butter, softened
⅔ cup granulated sugar	1¼ cups confectioners' sugar
1⅔ cups ground hazelnuts (filberts)	3 tbsp coffee liqueur
grated zest of 1 lemon	
1 tbsp chopped mixed candied peel	
1¼ sticks (5 oz) butter, melted and cooled	
1 quantity Chocolate Icing (page 120)	
melted white chocolate, to decorate	

Preheat the oven to 350°F. Butter and flour two 8 inch layer cake pans.

Melt the chocolate in a bowl over simmering water or in the top of a double boiler. Meanwhile, beat the egg yolks with the vanilla sugar and granulated sugar until light and fluffy. Beat in the hazelnuts, lemon zest and chopped mixed peel. Beat the melted chocolate and butter into the mixture. Beat the egg whites into stiff peaks and fold them into the mixture.

Divide the batter between the pans, and bake for 30 minutes or until a toothpick inserted in the centers comes out clean. Cool on wire racks.

To make the filling, melt the chocolate in a bowl over simmering water or the top of a double boiler. Beat the butter and sifted confectioners' sugar together until smooth, then beat in the liqueur and finally the melted chocolate. Sandwich the cakes together with the filling, then ice it with the chocolate icing. Pipe a decorative lacy pattern of melted white chocolate around the top edge of the cake.

Marble Cake

MARMORGUGELHUPF

This is another baking powder gugelhupf, and the favorite Austrian "everyday" coffee cake, quick and simple to make and very delicious. The recipe is courtesy of Mrs Lisl Ullmann.

SERVES 8–10

2 sticks (8 oz) butter, softened
1 cup granulated sugar
4 eggs, separated
1⅔ cups self-rising flour, sifted
grated zest of 1 lemon
¼ tsp salt
3 tbsp cocoa powder mixed with 3 tbsp granulated sugar
1 tbsp dark rum
¼ cup confectioners' sugar

Preheat the oven to 350°F. Thoroughly grease and flour one large or two small gugelhupf molds.

Beat the butter and granulated sugar together until light and fluffy. Beat in the egg yolks, then gradually beat in the flour. Add the lemon zest and salt. Beat the egg whites into stiff peaks and fold them gently but thoroughly into the mixture.

Put 8 heaped tbsp of the mixture into a separate bowl. Stir the cocoa and sugar mixture and the rum into this separate mixture.

Pour half the plain mixture into the prepared mold. Pour in the cocoa mixture, then top with the rest of the plain mixture. Bake for 50–60 minutes, or until well-browned on top.

Turn the gugelhupf upside-down on to a wire rack and carefully remove the mold. Sprinkle thickly with sifted confectioners' sugar, and allow to cool. This cake keeps for at least a week.

Illustrated on page 11

Bishop's Bread

BISCHOFSBROT

This cake is usually baked in a saddle of venison (rehrücken) mold, but it can also be baked in a 1½ quart capacity loaf pan. Equivalent amounts of other dried fruits and nuts can be substituted, including dates, raisins, glacé cherries, hazelnuts (filberts), walnuts, pistachios and pine nuts.

SERVES 10

6 eggs, separated
½ cup sugar
¾ cup all-purpose flour, sifted
1 cup sliced almonds
scant 1 cup golden raisins
grated zest and half the juice of 1 orange
⅓ cup chopped dried figs
⅓ cup chopped dried apricots
⅓ cup chopped candied peel
⅓ cup semisweet chocolate chips

Preheat the oven to 350°F. Grease and flour a rehrücken mold or loaf pan.

Beat the egg yolks with the sugar and flour. Mix in the almonds, raisins, orange zest and juice, figs, apricots, candied peel and chocolate chips. Beat the egg whites into stiff peaks and fold them gently but thoroughly into the mixture.

Pour the mixture into the prepared mold and bake for 1 hour. Leave it to cool in the mold for 5 minutes, then turn it out on to a wire rack to cool completely. Store for at least 24 hours before eating.

Illustrated on page 10

Red Currant Tart

RIBISELKUCHEN

Any berry fruit, or Morello cherries, can be baked in this tart. The dough can also be baked in individual tartlet tins.

SERVES 8–10

1 stick butter, chilled	***Red currant filling***
1¼ cups all-purpose flour, sifted	**2 lb red currants or other berries (about 6 cups)**
¼ cup sugar	**⅓ cup sugar**
1 tsp lemon juice	**2 egg whites**
1 egg yolk	

Combine the chilled butter with the flour and sugar, cutting and rubbing until the mixture resembles bread crumbs. Add the lemon juice and egg yolk and mix to a firm dough. If it is too dry to stick together, add a few drops of water. Wrap the dough and refrigerate for 20 minutes.

Preheat the oven to 375°F. Grease a loose-bottomed 9 inch tart or quiche mold, or 8 individual 2 inch tartlet tins.

Roll out the dough and use it to line the mold (or tins), trimming off any surplus dough with a knife. Line with foil, then sprinkle grains of raw rice or dried beans into the mold or tins and bake unfilled for 20 minutes or until lightly browned.

Remove from the oven and reduce the oven temperature to 275°F. Discard the foil and rice or beans and arrange the fruit thickly but evenly in the pastry case. Sprinkle with 1 tbsp of the sugar. Beat the egg whites into stiff peaks with 2 tbsp of the sugar, then fold in the rest of the sugar. Pile this meringue over the fruit. Bake for 30 minutes for a whole tart, 20 minutes for tartlets. Leave to cool completely before unmolding and serving.

Chocolate Wafer Cake

PISCHINGERTORTE

This cake, named after a famous Austrian pâtissier, is simple enough to be made by children. The large round wafers, called oblaten, can be replaced with other plain flat crackers, such as matzos, or you can use ice cream wafers, arranging them in circles.

SERVES 12

6 tbsp butter, softened
4 oz semisweet chocolate, melted
1 tsp ground cinnamon
2 eggs
½ cup vanilla sugar
1½ cups ground almonds
6 oblaten or substitutes
1 quantity Chocolate Icing (page 120)
12 shelled hazelnuts (filberts)

Beat the butter with the chocolate and cinnamon until smoothly blended, then beat in the eggs, sugar and ground almonds. Spread this cream over 5 of the oblaten and arrange them one on top of the other. Place the remaining wafer on top.

Coat with the chocolate icing, and score into 12 slices before the icing hardens. Decorate with the hazelnuts. Refrigerate overnight before serving.

Baking Powder Gugelhupf

BACKPULVERGUGELHUPF

The yeast dough mixture baked in the elegant ring mold, called a gugelhupf mold, is popular from Vienna to Alsace-Lorraine. This is largely because of the strong Austrian influence on that region of France due to the frequent marriages of local dukes with the Austrian nobility. This baking powder version is becoming increasingly popular, even in Austria, with cooks who do not have time to let the yeast doughs rise. For the classic gugelhupf *see pages 56–7.*

SERVES 10

6 tbsp butter, softened
¾ cup granulated sugar
5 eggs, 4 separated
grated zest of 1 lemon
2 cups all-purpose flour, sifted
½ cup milk
1 tsp baking powder
2 tbsp golden raisins
¼ cup confectioners' sugar

Preheat the oven to 350°F. Thoroughly grease and flour one large or two small gugelhupf molds.

Beat the butter until light and fluffy, then add the granulated sugar, 4 egg yolks and the whole egg, lemon zest, half the flour and the milk. Beat well. Sift the rest of the flour with the baking powder and stir this into the mixture. Beat the 4 egg whites into stiff peaks and fold them into the mixture. Stir in the raisins.

Pile the mixture into the prepared mold. Bake for 50–60 minutes or until the top is well browned. Turn the gugelhupf upside-down on to a wire rack and carefully remove the mold. Sprinkle thickly with sifted confectioners' sugar and leave to cool. This cake keeps well.

Yeast Dough Cakes

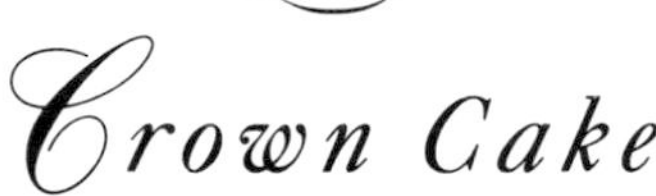

Crown Cake

KRANZKUCHEN

This cake is made with yeast puff dough, the invention of Viennese bakers. The English-speaking world calls pastries made with this dough Danish pastries because the Danes imported Viennese bakers to show them how to make it. However, in Denmark the pastry is known as wienerbrød, and in France as viennoiserie. What usually passes for Danish pastry is a pale shadow of the real thing, as you will soon discover when you make it yourself.

SERVES 12

1 quantity Yeast Puff Dough (page 119)
2 tbsp ground unblanched almonds or hazelnuts (filberts)
¼ cup golden raisins
1 oz semisweet chocolate, grated
1 graham cracker, crushed
1 tbsp sugar
2 tbsp rum
1 tbsp ground cinnamon
1 tbsp butter, melted
1 egg, lightly beaten
1 quantity Glacé Icing (page 121)

Roll out the yeast puff dough on a floured cloth into a rectangle about 8 × 10 inches. Combine the ground nuts, raisins, grated chocolate, cracker crumbs and sugar, and sprinkle the mixture over the dough. Sprinkle with the rum, cinnamon and melted butter.

Roll up the dough as for Austrian Jam Roll (page 44), and shape it into a ring. Slide the ring on to a greased baking sheet. Use a very sharp knife or razor blade to cut several diagonal slashes in the top. Leave the ring in a warm place to rise for about 45 minutes, or until the dough has puffed up slightly.

Preheat the oven to 400°F. Brush the dough with beaten egg. Bake for 25 minutes, then reduce the heat to 350°F and bake for a further 20 minutes.

Cool on a wire rack, and ice when cold.

Old-Fashioned Gugelhupf with Poppyseed Filling

PATZERLGUGELHUPF MIT MOHNFÜLLE

This famous Austrian cake has been exported all over the German-speaking world, even as far as Alsace-Lorraine, whose dukes married into the Austrian royal family. The name simply means "ball hoop," a reference to the elaborate ring-shaped mold in which it is baked. These molds are fairly easy to find in good cookware shops. They can be made of metal or even ovenproof china, but the best ones are made of tinned copper. They are available in a variety of sizes, from 1 pint to 1½ quarts. In view of this fact, no size is specified for the gugelhupf recipes in this book, but the quantity of mixture given is usually enough for one large mold or two small ones. Gugelhupf molds need to be greased very thoroughly, so that the mixture does not stick to the angles in the fancy molding. They should also be dusted with a dry ingredient. Flour can be used, but even more delicious are ground almonds or hazelnuts (filberts), or crushed graham crackers or even Spice Cookies (page 92).

SERVES 8–10

	Poppyseed filling
½ oz compressed yeast, or 1 package active dry yeast	¾ cup poppyseeds, freshly ground
¼ cup milk, at blood heat	1 tsp ground cinnamon
2 cups bread flour	3 tbsp milk
½ cup granulated sugar	¼ cup vanilla sugar
2 tbsp vanilla sugar	1 tbsp butter
¼ tsp salt	2 tbsp dark rum
2 eggs, beaten	
2 tbsp dark rum	
grated zest of 1 lemon	
6 tbsp butter, softened	
¼ cup confectioners' sugar	

Cream the compressed yeast with the milk, or stir dried yeast into the milk until dissolved, and leave in a warm place until foaming, about 20 minutes.

Sift the flour, granulated sugar, vanilla sugar and salt into the bowl of a heavy duty (countertop) electric mixer. Make a well in the center and add the eggs, rum and lemon zest. Gradually work in the flour using the dough hook, and when smooth gradually add the yeast mixture. Work until the dough is smooth and elastic. Work in the butter.

Cover the bowl with a dampened cloth and leave the dough in a warm place to rise until doubled in bulk, about 1½ hours.

Meanwhile, thoroughly grease one large or two small gugelhupf molds and dust with flour. To prepare the filling: put all the ingredients into a saucepan and cook, stirring constantly, over gentle heat until the butter has melted. Set aside to cool slightly.

Turn the dough out on to a lightly floured surface, punch down and knead until smooth and elastic again. Roll the dough into a thick sausage shape about 4 inches in diameter, and cut it into slices about 1 inch thick. Spread each slice with some of the filling, pressing it well down into the dough, then arrange the slices in overlapping layers in the mold so that all spaces between the slices are filled. The mold should be about half full. Cover it with a damp cloth again and put it in a warm place to rise again for about 1 hour, or until the dough has risen almost to the rim of the mold.

Preheat the oven to 350°F. Bake the gugelhupf for 50 minutes or until the top is well-browned and the cake slightly shrunk away from the sides of the mold. Leave it to cool in the mold for 5 minutes, then unmold it on to a wire rack. Sprinkle generously with sifted confectioners' sugar before serving.

Carinthian Gugelhupf

KÄRTNER GUGELHUPF

This type of gugelhupf is typical of Carinthia, Austria's southernmost province, where nuts grow in profusion. This simple version mixes the nuts straight into the dough, without adding them in a separate layer, but it is none the less delicious for that.

SERVES 8–10

½ oz compressed yeast, or 1 package active dry yeast
1 cup milk, at blood heat
2 cups bread flour
¼ tsp salt
1 stick unsalted butter
½ cup granulated sugar
3 eggs, 2 separated
¼ cup coarsely chopped blanched almonds
¼ cup coarsely chopped walnuts
¼ cup coarsely chopped hazelnuts (filberts)
1 tsp almond or bitter almond extract
grated zest of 1 lemon
¼ cup rum
¼ cup golden raisins
¼ cup ground almonds
6 tbsp confectioners' sugar

Cream the compressed yeast with the milk, or stir dried yeast into the milk until dissolved, and leave in a warm place until foaming, about 20 minutes.

Sift the flour and salt into a bowl. Beat the butter until it is creamy and add the flour and yeast mixture. Beat in the granulated sugar, whole egg, 2 egg yolks, chopped nuts, almond extract, lemon zest and rum. Work the batter until bubbles form. Beat the egg whites into stiff peaks and fold them into the batter. Add the sultanas.

Cover the bowl with a dampened cloth and leave the dough in a warm place to rise until doubled in bulk, about 1½ hours. Meanwhile, thoroughly grease a gugelhupf mold and dust it with the ground almonds.

Turn the dough out on to a lightly floured surface, punch down and knead until smooth and elastic again. Put the dough into the prepared mold, and cover it with a damp cloth. Put it in a warm place to rise again for about 1 hour, or until the dough has risen almost to the rim of the mold.

Preheat the oven to 350°F. Bake the gugelhupf for 1 hour or until the top is well browned and the cake slightly shrunk away from the sides of the mold. Leave it to cool in the mold for 5 minutes, then unmold it on to a wire rack. Sprinkle generously with sifted confectioners' sugar before serving.

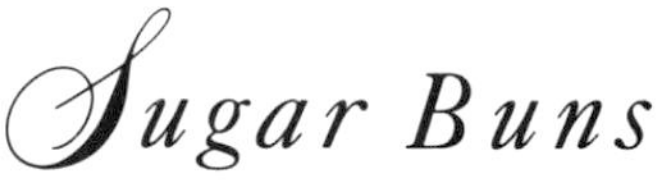

Sugar Buns

BUCHTELN

These buns originated from Czechoslovakia, and are now firmly entrenched at the Austrian table. You can substitute Yeast Puff Dough (page 119) for this dough.

MAKES ABOUT 24

½ oz compressed yeast, or 1 package active dry yeast
½ cup milk, at blood heat
1¾ cups bread flour
½ tsp salt
2 tbsp sugar
1 egg
2 sticks (8 oz) butter, melted
⅔ cup plum butter
6 tbsp confectioners' sugar

Cream the compressed yeast with the milk or stir dried yeast into the milk until dissolved, and leave in a warm place until foaming, about 20 minutes.

Sift the flour and salt into the bowl of a heavy duty (countertop) electric mixer. Add the sugar and stir in the yeast mixture. Beat in the egg and half the melted butter and work into a dough using the dough hook. Work the dough until it no longer sticks to the sides of the bowl or the beater, and it is smooth and elastic.

Cover the bowl with a cloth and leave the dough in a warm place to rise until doubled in bulk, about 1½ hours.

Turn the dough out on to a lightly floured surface, punch down and knead until smooth and elastic again. Roll out the dough into a rectangle about ¾ inch thick. Cut it into 3 × 2½ inch rectangles. Spread plum butter over one-third of each rectangle and roll them up like little jelly rolls.

Dip them in the rest of the melted butter and place them close together in 2 buttered roasting pans. Leave in a warm place until well risen, about 45 minutes.

Preheat the oven to 375°F. Pour any remaining melted butter over the buns and bake for 30 minutes or until well browned. Remove them from the pans while they are still hot and dust them liberally with sifted confectioners' sugar.

Nut or Poppyseed Crescents

NUSS- ODER MOHNKIPFERL

MAKES 20

½ oz compressed yeast, or 1 package active dry yeast
1 cup milk, at blood heat
1¾ sticks (7 oz) butter
3¼ cups bread flour, sifted
¼ tsp salt
2 egg yolks
2 tbsp heavy cream
1 quantity Nut Filling or Poppyseed Filling (page 124 or 123)
1 egg, lightly beaten

Cream the compressed yeast with 6 tbsp of the milk, or stir dried yeast into the milk until dissolved, and leave in a warm place until foaming, about 20 minutes.

Cut the butter into small pieces and rub it into the flour until the mixture resembles bread crumbs. Add the salt, egg yolks, cream, yeast mixture and enough of the remaining milk to form a stiff dough. Knead the dough until it is smooth and elastic and no longer sticks to the bowl or your fingers.

Roll out the dough on a lightly floured surface into a 12 × 4 inch rectangle. Fold over the long ends of the dough so they meet in the center. Turn the dough through 90° (a quarter circle), so that a short side of the rectangle faces you, then roll out the dough again, and fold the long ends toward the center. Repeat this process of rolling, folding and turning 4 times. Cover the dough and leave it in a warm place to rise for 1 hour or until it has doubled in bulk.

Punch down the dough and roll it out again into a rectangle about ¼ inch thick. Cut the dough into 20 squares. Put a teaspoon of the chosen filling into one corner of each dough square. Starting with the corner containing the filling, roll up the dough and curl the ends slightly, as if you were making croissants.

Transfer the crescents to 2 greased baking sheets and leave them to rise in a warm place for 45 minutes, or until puffed up.

Preheat the oven to 425°F. Brush the crescents with the beaten egg and bake them for 20 minutes or until well browned.

Illustrated on page 63

Yeast Marble Cake

MARMORGERMGUGELHUPF

SERVES 8–10

	Filling
½ oz compressed yeast, or 1 package active dry yeast	6 oz ginger snap cookies, crushed (about 2 cups)
1 cup milk, at blood heat	⅓ cup clear honey
4 cups bread flour	1 tbsp butter, melted
¼ tsp salt	¾ cup ground almonds
¾ cup granulated sugar	1 tbsp ground cinnamon mixed with 1 tbsp brown sugar
4 tbsp unsalted butter, melted	
2 eggs, lightly beaten	
4 egg yolks	
¼ tsp grated nutmeg	
1 tbsp chopped blanched almonds	
1 tsp almond extract	
grated zest of 1 lemon	
¼ cup ground almonds	
6 tbsp confectioners' sugar	

Cream the compressed yeast with the milk, or stir dried yeast into the milk until dissolved, and leave in a warm place until foaming, about 20 minutes.

Sift the flour, salt and granulated sugar into the bowl of a heavy duty (countertop) electric mixer. Add the butter, then beat in the yeast mixture, eggs, egg yolks, nutmeg, chopped almonds, almond extract and lemon zest, using the dough hook. Work the dough until it is smooth and elastic.

Cover the bowl with a dampened cloth and leave the dough in a warm place to rise until doubled in bulk, about 1½ hours. Meanwhile, thoroughly grease one large or two small gugelhupf molds and dust with the ground almonds.

Turn the dough out on to a lightly floured surface, punch down lightly and roll out into a 10 × 12 inch rectangle. Sprinkle the dough with the cookie crumbs, then dribble the honey over it evenly. Sprinkle with the melted butter and ground almonds, and finally with the cinnamon-and-sugar mixture. Roll it up like a jelly roll or a strudel (see page 42), coil it around and place it in the prepared gugelhupf mold.

Cover the mold with a damp cloth and put it in a warm place to rise again for about 1 hour, or until the dough has risen almost to the rim of the mold.

Preheat the oven to 350°F. Bake the gugelhupf for 1 hour or until the top is well browned and the cake slightly shrunk away from the sides of the mold. Leave it to cool in the mold for 5 minutes, then unmold it on to a wire rack. Sprinkle generously with sifted confectioners' sugar before serving.

Milk Bread

MILCHBROT

This is far from being a plain bread. It is often baked on Saturday evening for the following day, to be served instead of purchased bread on Sunday, since there is no night or Sunday baking in Austria.

SERVES 8–10

½ oz compressed yeast, or 1 package active dry yeast
¾ cup milk, at blood heat
2 cups bread flour
¼ tsp salt
grated zest of 1 lemon
3 tbsp butter, melted
¼ cup sugar
3 tbsp golden raisins
1 egg, beaten with 2 tsp water

Cream the compressed yeast with the milk, or stir dried yeast into the milk until dissolved, and leave in a warm place until foaming, about 20 minutes.

Sift the flour and salt into the bowl of a heavy duty (countertop) electric mixer. Add the grated lemon zest, melted butter, sugar and finally the yeast mixture. Work with the dough hook until smooth and elastic. Work in the raisins.

Cover the bowl with a dampened cloth and leave the dough in a warm place to rise until doubled in bulk, about 1½ hours.

Turn the dough out on to a lightly floured surface, punch down and knead until smooth and elastic again. Shape the dough into a round loaf and place it on a greased baking sheet. Leave it in a warm place to rise again for 45 minutes.

Preheat the oven to 400°F. Brush the loaf with the beaten egg mixture and bake for 1 hour, or until it sounds hollow when tapped on the base. Cool it on a wire rack. Serve with coffee.

Poppyseed Crescents & Milk Bread

Wasps' Nests

WESPENNESTER

MAKES ABOUT 20

½ oz compressed yeast, or 1 package active dry yeast
¾ cup milk, at blood heat
2 tbsp butter
1 egg yolk
¼ cup sugar
¼ tsp salt
1 tbsp grated lemon zest
2¼ cups bread flour, sifted
¾ cup sliced almonds
2 tbsp chopped candied citron peel or mixed peel
2 tbsp raisins
½ tsp ground cinnamon
2 tbsp semisweet chocolate chips
1 stick butter, melted

Cream the compressed yeast with the milk, or stir dried yeast into the milk until dissolved, and leave in a warm place until foaming, about 20 minutes.

Cream the butter in the bowl of a heavy duty (countertop) electric mixer. Beat in the egg yolk, sugar, salt and lemon zest. Work in the flour and yeast mixture alternately using the dough hook. Continue working until the dough comes away cleanly from the sides of the bowl, and it is smooth and elastic. Cover the bowl lightly with a damp cloth and leave the dough to rise in a warm place until doubled in bulk, about 1 hour.

Turn the dough out on to a lightly floured surface, punch down and knead until smooth and elastic again. Divide the dough in half.

Roll out each piece on the lightly floured board into a rectangle about 8 × 10 inches. Combine the almonds, peel, raisins, cinnamon and chocolate chips, and sprinkle each piece with half the mixture. Roll up each piece like a jelly roll. Cut the rolls crosswise into slices 2 inches thick, and dip them in the melted butter. Arrange them, cut side down, in a shallow baking pan or jelly roll pan in which they will fit comfortably. Cover lightly with a cloth and leave them in a warm place to rise again for 45 minutes.

Preheat the oven to 350°F. Bake the Wasps' Nests for 30 minutes.

Yeast Crumb Cake

HEFETEIGSTREUSELKUCHEN

Baking powder doughs are also used for Crumb Cake, but the technique is basically the same: a cake or pastry base, sometimes topped with fruit or jam, and sprinkled with the crumb mixture. For many people, Crumb Cake is one of the most typical products of Austrian home baking.

MAKES 16 SLICES

	Crumb topping
½ oz compressed yeast, or 1 package active dry yeast	1 cup all-purpose flour, sifted
½ cup milk, at blood heat	½ cup ground almonds
1⅔ cups bread flour	1 tsp grated lemon zest
½ tsp salt	¼ tsp ground cinnamon
3 egg yolks	6 tbsp sugar
2 tbsp butter, softened	5 tbsp butter, melted
1 tbsp sugar	
½ tsp grated lemon zest	

Cream the compressed yeast with the milk, or stir dried yeast into the milk until dissolved, and leave in a warm place until foaming, about 20 minutes.

Sift the flour and salt into the bowl of a heavy duty (countertop) electric mixer. Make a well in the center and add the egg yolks, butter, sugar and grated lemon zest. Stir to combine, then gradually stir in the yeast mixture. Work the dough with the dough hook until it no longer sticks to the sides of the bowl or the beater, and it is smooth and elastic. Cover the bowl with a cloth and leave in a warm place to rise until doubled in bulk, about 1½ hours.

Turn the dough out on to a lightly floured surface, punch down and knead until smooth and elastic again. Roll out the dough to about ¼ inch thick and press it over a greased baking sheet. Leave it to rise again in a warm place for 45 minutes.

Preheat the oven to 350°F. Prepare the crumb topping: combine the dry ingredients, then add the butter, and rub with your fingertips until the mixture has the consistency of bread crumbs.

Sprinkle the topping over the dough and bake for 45 minutes.

Jam, Poppyseed Filling (page 123), Nut Filling (page 124) or soft berry fruits such as blueberries may be spread over the dough before adding the crumbs.

Christmas Braid

WEIHNACHTSSTRIEZL

If you find it too hard to make a 4-strand braid, divide the dough into nine portions and make three 3-strand braids. The dough strands can also be simply twisted and laid on top of each other.

SERVES 10–12

½ oz compressed yeast, or 1 package active dry yeast
¾ cup milk, at blood heat
4 cups bread flour
¼ tsp salt
grated zest of 1 lemon
¼ tsp grated nutmeg
1 tsp almond or bitter almond extract
1 egg
2 egg yolks
1 stick butter, softened
¾ cup sugar
1 cup chopped blanched almonds
scant 1 cup raisins
1 egg white, lightly beaten
1 quantity Glacé Icing (page 121)

Cream the compressed yeast with the milk, or stir dried yeast into the milk until dissolved, and leave in a warm place until foaming, about 20 minutes.

Sift the flour and salt into the bowl of a heavy duty (countertop) electric mixer. Add the lemon zest, nutmeg, almond extract, whole egg, egg yolks, softened butter, sugar and finally the yeast mixture. Work with the dough hook until smooth and elastic. Work in the almonds and raisins.

Cover the bowl with a dampened cloth and leave the dough in a warm place to rise until doubled in bulk, about 1½ hours.

Turn the dough out on to a floured board, punch down and knead until smooth and elastic again. Divide it into 7 portions, 4 slightly bigger than the other 3. Roll each portion into a sausage shape 12 inches long. Take the 4 thicker sausages and braid them, then do the same with the 3 thinner ones. Lay the 3-strand braid on top of the 4-strand braid and fasten together with wooden toothpicks.

Butter and flour a baking sheet and carefully transfer the braided loaf to it. Leave it in a warm place to rise again for 45 minutes.

Preheat the oven to 400°F. Brush the loaf with the beaten egg white and bake for 1 hour, or until it sounds hollow when tapped on the base. Cool it on a wire rack.

Drizzle the icing over it when it is cold. Keep it for 48 hours before serving.

Carnival Doughnuts

FASCHINGSKRAPFEN

MAKES ABOUT 20

½ oz compressed yeast, or 1 package active dry yeast
¼ cup water, at blood heat
2½ cups bread flour
¼ tsp salt
2 tbsp vanilla sugar
6 egg yolks
6 tbsp light cream, at room temperature
1 tbsp dark rum
grated zest and half the juice of 1 orange
1 lb (1⅓ cups) raspberry or plum jam
oil for deep-frying
½ cup confectioners' sugar

Cream the compressed yeast with the water, or stir dried yeast into the water until dissolved, and leave in a warm place until foaming, about 20 minutes.

Sift the flour and salt into a bowl. Make a well in the center and pour in the vanilla sugar, egg yolks, cream, rum, orange zest and juice. Beat the mixture with a wooden spoon, gradually adding the yeast mixture. Continue beating the dough with a spoon or your hand until it is smooth and shiny and no longer sticks to the sides of the bowl.

Butter a large bowl, put the dough into it and dust it with flour. Cover it with a damp cloth and leave it in a warm place to rise until doubled in bulk, about 1 hour.

Punch down the dough, and turn it on to a well-floured work surface. Roll it out into a rectangle about ¼ inch thick. Use a glass or plain cookie cutter to cut out rounds about 2 inches in diameter. Roll the dough trimmings into a ball, roll them out again and cut more rounds, until all the dough has been used.

Drop a teaspoon of jam on to the center of half the rounds. Cover each jam round with a plain round and press the edges of the rounds together with your fingertips.

Line 2 baking sheets with nonstick parchment paper and dust them with flour. Arrange the dough rounds on the baking sheets and leave in a warm place to rise again for about 40 minutes, or until they have risen by about ½ inch and look puffy.

Heat oil in a deep-fryer until it is hot enough for a cube of stale bread to brown in 60 seconds (350°F on a thermometer). Use a spatula to slide the doughnuts, 3 or 4 at a time, into the oil and fry them for 2 minutes, or until they have puffed up and are browned on the bottom. Turn them over with a slotted spoon and fry for another 2 minutes or until browned. Drain the doughnuts on paper towels.

Sprinkle thickly with sifted confectioners' sugar and serve while still warm.

Fruitbread

FRUCHTBROT

MAKES 3 LOAVES (SERVES 25)

1 lb dried figs, diced (about 3½ cups)
½ lb dried dates, pitted and chopped (about 1½ cups)
½ lb dried pears, chopped (about 1½ cups)
½ lb prunes, pitted and chopped (about 1½ cups)
½ lb raisins, chopped
scant 1 cup chopped mixed candied peel
1 cup coarsely chopped walnuts
1 cup coarsely chopped hazelnuts (filberts)
1 tbsp ground cinnamon
¼ tsp ground cloves
¼ cup dark rum
½ oz compressed yeast, or 1 package active dry yeast
6 tbsp water, at blood heat
¾ cup bread flour, sifted
1 tbsp wine vinegar
¼ tsp salt
3 oblaten (wafers), or 3 sheets rice paper
1 egg, lightly beaten
1 cup blanched almonds, halved
¼ cup light corn syrup

Mix the dried fruit, peel and chopped nuts with the spices and rum and leave the mixture in a cool place to macerate overnight.

The next day cream the compressed yeast with ¼ cup of the water, or stir dried yeast into the water until dissolved, and leave in a warm place until foaming, about 20 minutes.

Stir the yeast mixture into the flour. Add the vinegar and salt and leave the dough in a warm place for 30 minutes to rise.

Line 3 baking sheets with oblaten or sheets of rice paper. Preheat the oven to 300°F.

Add the yeast dough to the fruit mixture and beat well. Shape the mixture into 3 oblong loaves and arrange them over the wafers or rice paper. Brush them with the beaten egg and scatter over the halved almonds. Bake the loaves for 1 hour.

Mix the corn syrup with the rest of the water and brush the mixture over the loaves. Return them to the oven and bake them for another 45 minutes, brushing them twice more with the corn syrup mixture during that time.

Cream Cheese Buns

TOPFENKOLATSCHEN

These buns are the original version of what is known as a "cheese Danish." It is only by making them at home that you realize how unfavorably the purchased version compares with your own creation. For a richer version, use the Yeast Puff Dough on page 119.

MAKES 10

½ oz compressed yeast, or 1 package active dry yeast	***Cream cheese filling***
½ cup milk, at blood heat	**2 tbsp butter, softened**
1¾ cups bread flour	**½ lb medium-fat cream cheese (about 1 cup)**
½ tsp salt	**2 eggs, separated**
2 tbsp sugar	**½ cup sugar**
1 egg	**grated zest of 1 lemon**
2 tbsp butter, melted	**1 tbsp golden raisins**
1 egg white, lightly beaten	
2 tbsp ground or chopped almonds	

Cream the compressed yeast with the milk, or stir dried yeast into the milk until dissolved, and leave in a warm place until foaming, about 20 minutes.

Sift the flour and salt into the bowl of a heavy duty (countertop) electric mixer. Add the sugar and stir in the yeast mixture. Beat in the egg and the melted butter and work into a dough using a wooden spoon or the dough hook. Work the dough until it no longer sticks to the sides of the bowl or the beater, and it is smooth and elastic.

Cover the bowl with a cloth and leave the dough in a warm place to rise until doubled in bulk, about 1½ hours.

Turn the dough out on to a lightly floured surface, punch down and knead until smooth and elastic again. Roll out the dough into a rectangle about ½ inch thick. Cut it into 3 inch squares. Arrange the squares on greased baking sheets about 1 inch apart.

To make the filling, combine the butter, cream cheese, egg yolks, sugar and lemon zest in a food processor, fitted with the metal blade, and process until smooth. Beat the egg whites until stiff and fold them into the mixture. Stir in the raisins.

Put a tablespoon of filling in the center of each square of dough and fold the corners toward the center, pressing them together lightly to hold in the filling. Leave the buns to rise again in a warm place for about 45 minutes.

Preheat the oven to 400°F. Brush the buns with the egg white and sprinkle them with the ground or chopped almonds. Bake for 30 minutes or until well browned.

Chocolate-Filled Yeast Roll

GERMROULADE MIT SCHOKOLADENFÜLLUNG

This type of yeast dough is very popular in home baking. It can be filled with any of the strudel fillings for which recipes are given on pages 122–3. The most commonly used are poppyseed and nut, but this chocolate version is also very popular. The poppyseed version is often iced with glacé icing. The chocolate version is merely glazed with egg.

MAKES 30 SLICES

	Chocolate filling
½ oz compressed yeast, or 1 package active dry yeast	6 tbsp cocoa powder
½ cup milk, at blood heat	¾ cup sugar
2¼ cups bread flour	1 tbsp ground cinnamon
¼ tsp salt	scant 1 cup raisins
1 tbsp sugar	4 tbsp butter, cut into small pieces
1 stick butter, softened	
1 egg, lightly beaten with 2 tsp water	

Cream the compressed yeast with the milk, or stir dried yeast into the milk until dissolved, and leave in a warm place until foaming, about 20 minutes.

Sift the flour and salt into the warmed bowl of a heavy duty (countertop) electric mixer.

Add the sugar and softened butter, and finally the yeast mixture. Work with the dough hook until smooth and elastic.

Cover the bowl with plastic wrap and leave the dough in a warm place to rise for about 1½ hours. As this dough is very firm, it will not rise much.

Turn the dough out on to a lightly floured surface, punch down and knead until smooth and elastic again. Roll out to an 8 × 10 inch rectangle. Sprinkle the cocoa evenly over the surface, leaving a ½ inch border all around the edge so that the filling does not escape. Sprinkle the cocoa evenly with the sugar and the cinnamon, then add the raisins. Dot with the small pieces of butter. Roll up the dough like a jelly roll.

Slide the roll carefully on to a buttered baking sheet, seam downward, and leave it in a warm place to rise again for 1 hour.

Preheat the oven to 400°F. Brush the dough with the beaten egg. Bake for 10 minutes, then reduce the heat to 375°F and bake for 30 minutes longer. Cool the roll on the baking sheet. Cut into slices when cold.

Slices & Bars

Plum Slices

PFLAUMENSCHNITTEN

Do not use large plums for this recipe; they will not only weigh down the dough and look unattractive but will not cook through in the specified time.

MAKES 12

2 sticks (8 oz) butter, softened
4 eggs
1 cup granulated sugar
1 tsp grated orange zest
1 tsp grated lemon zest
½ tsp ground cinnamon
1 tbsp rum
1¼ cups all-purpose flour, sifted
1 lb ripe sweet plums
¼ cup confectioners' sugar

Preheat the oven to 325°F. Butter and flour a 10 × 12 inch jelly roll pan.

Cream the butter with the eggs and sugar until smooth. Add the grated zests, cinnamon and rum, and continue beating until smooth. Beat in the flour and blend well.

Spread the mixture in the jelly roll pan, smoothing it down lightly. Slice the plums neatly in half and remove the pits. Place the halves, cut side down, at regular intervals over the mixture.

Bake for 20 minutes. Remove from the oven and sprinkle immediately with sifted confectioners' sugar. Score into 2 inch wide slices, and serve hot or cold.

Date Bars

DATTELBÜSSERLN

MAKES ABOUT 10

3 egg whites
1 cup sugar
½ lb pitted dried dates, chopped (about 1½ cups)
¾ cup chopped walnuts
2 tbsp chopped candied citron peel or mixed peel

Preheat the oven to 225°F. Cover an 8 × 10 inch baking sheet with rice paper.

Beat the egg whites to soft peaks. Gradually beat in one-third of the sugar, and continue beating until stiff. Fold in the rest of the sugar, and the dates, walnuts and peel.

Spread the mixture over the rice paper and bake for 1½ hours. Turn off the oven and let the mixture cool inside it for another hour. Cut into bars while still warm. Cool completely before serving.

Corsicans

KORSIKANER

MAKES 16

4 tbsp butter, softened
1⅔ cups all-purpose flour, sifted
1 cup sugar
1 tsp ground allspice
1 tsp grated lemon zest
¾ cup unblanched ground hazelnuts (filberts)
2 eggs
1 egg white, very lightly beaten

Preheat the oven to 375°F. Grease a 10 × 12 inch baking sheet.

Combine the butter with the flour, sugar, allspice, lemon zest, nuts and whole eggs, to make a dough. Roll out the dough on a lightly floured surface to a thickness of ⅛ inch and transfer it to the baking sheet. Use a sharp knife or pastry wheel to cut the dough into strips about 1 × 2 inches. Brush the strips with the egg white. Bake for 10 minutes. Cool on the baking sheet before transferring to a wire rack.

Bee Sting Slices & Chestnut Squares

Napoleons

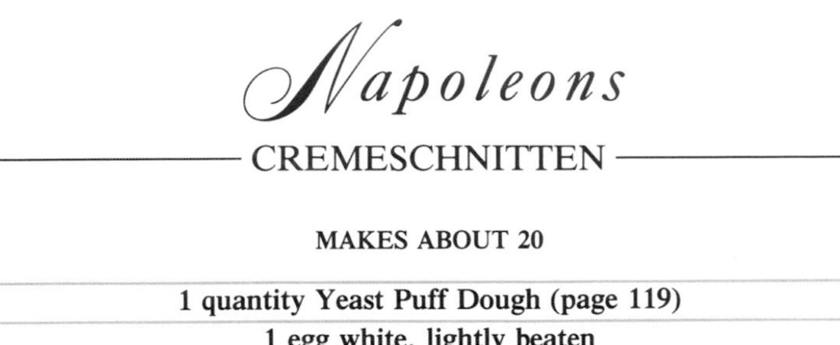

Napoleons

CREMESCHNITTEN

MAKES ABOUT 20

1 quantity Yeast Puff Dough (page 119)
1 egg white, lightly beaten
1 quantity Vanilla Cream (page 124)
1 quantity Fondant Icing (page 121)

Preheat the oven to 475°F. Sprinkle a large baking sheet with water.

Roll out the yeast puff dough on a lightly floured surface into a rectangle ¼ inch thick and place it on the baking sheet. Brush with the egg white, and bake for 10 minutes or until lightly browned.

Remove the pastry from the oven and cut it in half lengthwise. Leave to cool.

When cold, spread one of the pastry strips with the vanilla cream. Cut the second pastry strip into 2 × 4 inch rectangles and place them close together on top of the cream, to reassemble the strip. Slice through to the bottom layer, so you have cream "sandwiches."

Ice with fondant icing, thinned down with water so that it can be drizzled over the slices.

Bee Sting Slices

BIENENSTICHE

MAKES 30

1¾ cups all-purpose flour	***Almond topping***
¼ tsp baking powder	**1 stick butter**
3 tbsp granulated sugar	**¼ cup vanilla sugar**
1 stick butter, softened	**½ cup ground almonds**
3 tbsp milk	
confectioners' sugar	

Grease and flour a jelly roll pan. Sift the flour, baking powder and granulated sugar into a bowl. Beat in the softened butter and milk and work into a smooth dough. Cover and refrigerate for 30 minutes.

Preheat the oven to 350°F. Roll out the dough on a lightly floured surface until it is ¼ inch thick and use it to line the jelly roll pan.

To make the topping, melt the butter and stir in the vanilla sugar and ground almonds over low heat until the mixture is smooth and creamy. Remove it from the heat and stir until it is thickened and cooled.

Pour the topping over the dough, and bake for 40 minutes or until lightly browned and set. Cut into slices to serve, dusted with sifted confectioners' sugar.

Chestnut Squares

KASTANIENWÜRFEL

Chestnut purée can be bought in cans, but you can make your own at home by boiling shelled and peeled chestnuts in milk to cover with a vanilla bean until soft, then draining and puréeing in a food processor or by hand in a vegetable mill. You will need about 3lb chestnuts for this recipe. Set a small amount of the chestnut purée aside and sweeten it with sifted confectioners' sugar to taste for the decoration.

MAKES 18

¾ lb unsweetened chestnut purée (about 2 cups)	***Chestnut filling***
¾ cup sugar	**1 cup heavy cream**
6 eggs, separated	**¼ cup confectioners' sugar**
scant ½ cup grated semisweet chocolate	**½ lb chestnut purée (about 1⅓ cups)**
1 tbsp all-purpose flour	
2 tbsp plum jam	
1 quantity Chocolate Icing (page 120)	
silver candy balls	
sweetened chestnut purée, to decorate	

Preheat the oven to 350°F. Line a 9 × 12 inch jelly roll pan with nonstick parchment paper.

Beat the chestnut purée with the sugar and egg yolks until smooth. Beat in the chocolate and flour. Beat the egg whites into stiff peaks and fold them into the mixture.

Spread the mixture ½ inch thick in the paper-lined pan, and bake for 20 minutes. Cut into 36 squares and remove from the paper. Cool on wire racks.

To make the chestnut filling: whip the cream with the sifted confectioners' sugar, and gradually beat in the chestnut purée.

Spread the filling over half the baked squares and cover with the remaining squares. Spread a layer of jam on top of the chestnut "sandwiches" and glaze with chocolate icing. Decorate with silver balls and sweetened chestnut purée.

Illustrated on pages 74–5

Gipsy Slices

ZIGEUNERSCHNITTEN

MAKES 24

1 oz semisweet chocolate	***Parisian cream***
1 tbsp butter	**2 oz semisweet chocolate, grated**
2 eggs	**⅔ cup heavy cream**
¼ cup sugar	
¼ cup all-purpose flour	
1 quantity Chocolate Icing (page 120)	

Preheat the oven to 400°F. Line a jelly roll pan with buttered nonstick parchment paper.

Melt the chocolate in a bowl over simmering water. Add the butter and stir until the mixture is smooth. Remove from the heat and reserve.

Put the eggs and sugar into the top of a double boiler or large bowl and whisk over gently simmering water until the mixture thickens. Remove from the heat and whisk until the mixture cools. Fold in the sifted flour, then stir in the chocolate-and-butter mixture.

Spread the mixture in a layer about ½ inch thick in the paper-lined pan. Bake for 20 minutes. While still warm, cut the sponge into 48 slices about 2 × 1½ inches. Remove the slices from the paper and cool on wire racks.

To make the Parisian cream: put the grated chocolate into a heavy-based saucepan with the cream and cook over low heat, stirring constantly. As the mixture comes to a boil it will start to rise; when it does so, remove it from the heat, and stir until it cools. Pour it into a bowl and leave to cool to room temperature. Refrigerate until thoroughly chilled, then whisk it until it just holds a soft peak. Chill again for 30 minutes.

Spread the cream over half the sponge slices and top with the other half. Ice with chocolate icing.

Cream Cheese Slices

TOPFENSCHNITTEN

Instead of the traditionally rich and fattening sour cream and cream cheese, these slices are just as good made with thick plain yogurt and medium-fat curd cheese, and are also more economical. If using cottage cheese, it should be sieved first.

MAKES 30

1¾ cups all-purpose flour	***Cream cheese filling***
2 sticks (8 oz) butter, softened	**¾ lb cream cheese (about 1½ cups), at room temperature**
1 egg	**3 tbsp butter, softened**
1 tbsp rum	**2 eggs, separated**
2 tbsp sour cream	**2 tbsp vanilla sugar**
2 tbsp sugar	**grated zest of 1 lemon**
1 egg, lightly beaten with 2 tsp water	**¼ cup sour cream**
1 quantity Glacé Icing (page 121)	**⅔ cup golden raisins**

Sift the flour into a bowl and add the butter, egg, rum, sour cream and sugar. Beat until you have a firm, smooth dough. Shape the dough into a ball, wrap and refrigerate for 30 minutes.

Preheat the oven to 350°F. On a well-floured surface, roll out half the dough and use it to cover a floured baking sheet. Roll out the other half of the dough and lay on another floured baking sheet. Bake the dough sheets for 15 minutes or until just starting to color.

Meanwhile make the filling: cream the cheese until smooth, then beat in the butter and egg yolks until fluffy. Beat in the vanilla sugar, lemon zest and sour cream, and stir in the raisins. Beat the egg whites into stiff peaks and fold them into the mixture.

Spread the filling over one pastry sheet. Carefully remove the other pastry sheet from its baking sheet and lay it on top of the filling. Brush it with the beaten egg. Return to the oven and bake until lightly browned, about 15 minutes. Cool on the baking sheet, then cut into bars and ice with glacé icing.

Small Cakes, Cookies & Pastries

Ischl Tartlets

ISCHLERTÖRTCHEN

These little tarts are named after a popular resort in the Austrian Alps, where the Emperor Franz-Josef had his summer residence.

MAKES ABOUT 20

1⅔ cups all-purpose flour, sifted
2½ sticks (10 oz) butter, softened
¾ cup granulated sugar
1½ cups ground almonds
½ tsp ground cinnamon
3 tbsp strawberry jam, sieved
3 tbsp apricot jam, sieved
2 tbsp confectioners' sugar

Preheat the oven to 350°F.

Beat the flour, butter, granulated sugar, almonds and cinnamon into a stiff dough. Roll it out on a lightly floured surface until it is ⅛ inch thick. Cut the dough into an equal number of shapes, using a decorative pastry cutter if liked. Use a smaller pastry cutter or glass to cut a hole out of the center of half the shapes. The heart shapes illustrated in the photograph look particularly attractive.

Transfer all the dough shapes to greased baking sheets and bake for 15 minutes; do not allow them to brown. Transfer to wire racks to cool. Place ½ tsp of strawberry jam in the center of half of the shapes without holes. Place ½ tsp of apricot jam in the center of the remaining whole cookies. Place the shapes with holes over the top so the jam shows through. Dust with sifted confectioners' sugar.

Illustrated on page 83

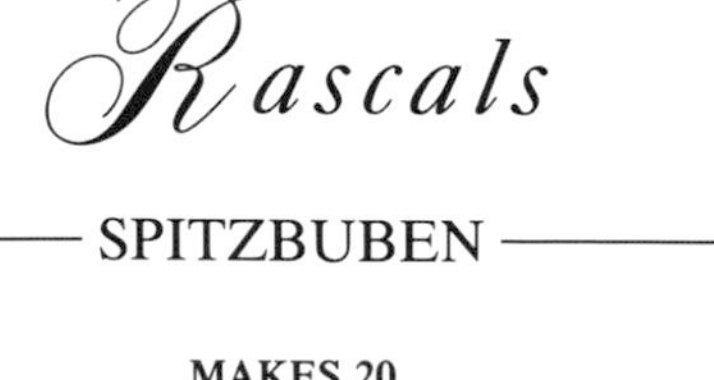

SPITZBUBEN

MAKES 20

2 sticks (8 oz) butter, softened
2 cups all-purpose flour, sifted
½ cup vanilla sugar
½ tsp grated lemon zest
1 egg, separated
1 extra egg yolk
⅔ cup plum butter or strawberry jam

Preheat the oven to 325°F.

Combine the butter, flour, vanilla sugar, lemon zest and 2 egg yolks to make a dough. Roll it out on a lightly floured surface until it is about ¼ inch thick. Use a cookie cutter to cut it into stars, rounds or other shapes, making sure you have an even number of each shape.

Place the shapes on greased baking sheets and brush with the lightly beaten egg white. Bake for 20 minutes or until lightly browned. Cool on wire racks.

Spread half of the cookies with plum butter or jam. Arrange the other half on top, to make cookie "sandwiches." Brush the tops with egg white and sprinkle with granulated sugar.

Illustrated on page 82

Sour Cream Muffins

RAHMDALKERLN

MAKES 6

¾ cup all-purpose flour, sifted
1 cup sour cream
4 eggs, separated
2 tbsp granulated sugar
2 tbsp confectioners' sugar

Preheat the oven to 400°F.

Beat the flour into the sour cream, then beat in the egg yolks, one by one, followed by the granulated sugar. Beat the egg whites into stiff peaks and fold them into the mixture.

Spoon into greased muffin tins, and bake for 25 minutes or until golden. Sprinkle with the sifted confectioners' sugar while still warm. Eat with butter and jam.

Rascals & Ischl Tartlets

Cloister Crescents

KLOSTERKIPFERLN

MAKES 10

1 stick butter, softened
¾ cup all-purpose flour, sifted
3 tbsp grated semisweet chocolate
¾ cup ground hazelnuts (filberts) or almonds
3 tbsp vanilla sugar
1 egg yolk
chocolate glaze for Little Indian Cakes (page 97)
2 tbsp chopped pistachio nuts

Preheat the oven to 350°F.

Beat the butter, flour, chocolate, nuts, vanilla sugar and egg yolk together to make a smooth, firm dough. Shape into a ball, wrap and refrigerate for 20 minutes.

Shape the dough into small crescents by pinching off walnut-sized pieces, rolling them into sausage-shapes and then bending them around. Arrange them on an ungreased baking sheet.

Bake the crescents for 15 minutes; do not allow them to color. Leave them to cool for 10 minutes on the baking sheet, then transfer them to a wire rack. Coat them with chocolate glaze and sprinkle evenly with the pistachio nuts.

Illustrated on page 86

Little Viennese Pockets

WIENERTASCHERLN

You can also fill these pockets with any of the strudel fillings or the nut filling on page 124. If you use the nut filling, the pockets would be delicious iced with spicy icing (page 120).

MAKES ABOUT 40

2¾ cups all-purpose flour, sifted
2 sticks (8 oz) butter, softened
½ cup vanilla sugar
1 tsp grated lemon zest
1 tbsp dark rum
2 hard-cooked egg yolks
1 egg, separated
⅔ cup blackberry jam or plum butter
1 quantity Glacé Icing (page 121)

Preheat the oven to 350°F.

Combine the flour, butter, vanilla sugar, lemon zest and rum. Rub the cooked egg yolks through a sieve over the mixture and stir them in with the yolk of the raw egg. Knead the mixture into a firm dough. Wrap and chill for 30 minutes.

On a well-floured surface, roll out the dough until it is ⅛ inch thick. Cut it into 3 inch squares. Place 1 tsp jam in the center of each square. Fold the corners of each square toward the center, and press lightly together over the jam. Beat the egg white lightly and brush it over the squares.

Transfer the pockets to greased baking sheets, and bake for 25 minutes or until golden brown. Cool on wire racks, and drizzle on glacé icing when cold.

Illustrated on page 87

Cloister Crescents & Sweet Pretzels

Little Viennese Pockets

Sweet Pretzels

NONNENBRETZERLN

The dough for these delicious pretzels is sometimes divided into two portions: one is then flavored with cinnamon and the two are twisted together before baking.

MAKES ABOUT 25

2 tbsp butter, softened
1 egg
½ cup confectioners' sugar, sifted
½ cup heavy cream
1¼ cups all-purpose flour, sifted
1 egg white, lightly beaten
6 tbsp confectioners' sugar, to dredge

Beat the butter with the egg, confectioners' sugar and cream. Work in the flour to make a smooth dough. Wrap and refrigerate for at least 30 minutes. Grease and flour 2 baking sheets.

Preheat the oven to 400°F. Break off walnut-sized pieces of dough and roll them into sausages. Shape the sausages into twisted figures of eight. Arrange on the baking sheets and brush with the egg white.

Bake for 20 minutes or until starting to color. Leave to cool before sprinkling with confectioners' sugar.

Illustrated on page 86

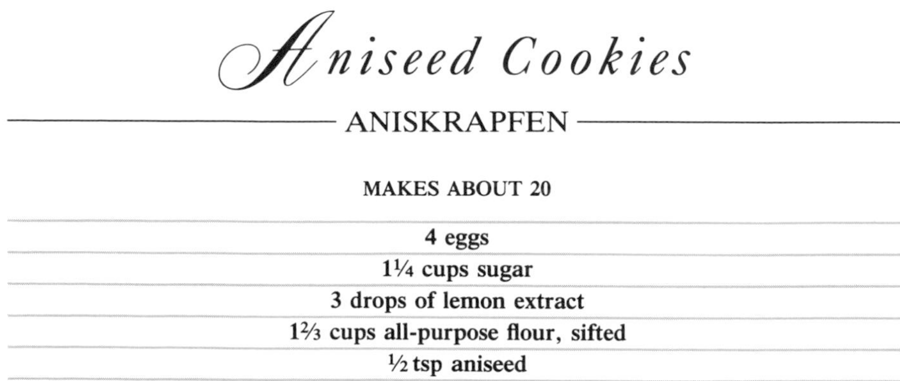

Aniseed Cookies

ANISKRAPFEN

MAKES ABOUT 20

4 eggs
1¼ cups sugar
3 drops of lemon extract
1⅔ cups all-purpose flour, sifted
½ tsp aniseed

Beat the eggs and sugar together until light and fluffy. Add the lemon extract and beat in the flour. Put the mixture into a pastry bag and pipe small rounds of it on to well-greased baking sheets. Leave in a warm place for at least 4 hours or overnight.

Preheat the oven to 300°F. Sprinkle the cookies with the aniseed and bake for 20 minutes or until just starting to color.

Carlsbad Rings

KARLSBADERRINGERLN

MAKES ABOUT 30

3 sticks (12 oz) butter, softened
6 tbsp granulated sugar
1 tsp grated lemon zest
1 egg yolk
3 hard-cooked egg yolks, sieved
1⅔ cups all-purpose flour, sifted
1 egg, beaten
½ cup chopped blanched almonds
1 tbsp vanilla sugar

Cream the butter with the granulated sugar. Add the grated lemon zest, raw egg yolk, hard-cooked egg yolks and flour. Knead briefly into a firm dough. Wrap the dough and refrigerate for 1 hour.

Preheat the oven to 350°F.

Roll out the dough on a lightly floured surface and cut it into rings using two pastry cutters, one of them 1 inch wider in diameter than the other (or a water glass and a liqueur glass). Reroll the centers and dough trimmings to make more rings until all the dough is used up. Brush the rings with the beaten egg, then sprinkle with the chopped almonds and then with the vanilla sugar.

Place the rings on greased baking sheets. Bake for 20 minutes or until the rings are just turning brown. Cool on wire racks.

Vanilla Crescents

VANILLEKIPFERLN

MAKES 20

1 cup all-purpose plain flour
1 stick unsalted butter
½ cup ground almonds
2 tbsp granulated sugar
about 2 cups confectioners' sugar

Preheat the oven to 300°F.

Sift the flour into a bowl. Cut the butter into pieces and rub or cut it into the flour until the mixture resembles fine bread crumbs. Add the almonds and granulated sugar, and mix to a firm dough.

Knead the dough briefly, then break off a walnut-sized piece. Roll it into a sausage shape about 1 inch thick and pinch the ends. Place it on a greased and floured baking sheet and curve the ends around to form crescents. Repeat with the rest of the dough.

Bake the crescents for 30 minutes; they should be barely starting to color. Meanwhile, dredge a sheet of wax paper with the sifted confectioners' sugar. As soon as you remove the cookies from the oven, roll them in the confectioners' sugar to coat them thickly. Leave them to cool on wire racks.

Widow's Kisses

WITWENKÜSSE

MAKES ABOUT 15

4 egg whites
¾ cup superfine sugar
2 cups coarsely chopped hazelnuts (filberts)
⅔ cup finely chopped candied citron peel

Preheat the oven to 250°F. Line an 8 × 10 inch baking sheet with rice paper.

Put the egg whites and sugar into the top of a double boiler or a large bowl and beat over hot water on gentle heat until the mixture thickens. Remove from the heat and continue to beat until the mixture is cold. Fold in the nuts and peel.

Use 2 teaspoons to shape the mixture into small rounds and lay them carefully on the rice paper. Bake for 15 minutes; do not allow to brown. Cool on wire racks. Separate the cookies when cold.

Store in an airtight tin lined with wax paper.

Widow's Kisses

Spice Cookies

LEBKUCHEN

These famous spiced honey cakes are traditionally eaten at Christmas. Because they contain no fat, they will keep for months. Do not omit the black pepper, which adds a unique spiciness, but make sure it is very finely ground.

MAKES 40

5 cups rye flour
½ tsp baking powder
½ tsp ground allspice
½ tsp ground cloves
¼ tsp grated nutmeg
1 tbsp ground cinnamon
½ tbsp freshly ground black pepper
grated zest of 1 lemon
grated zest of ½ orange
4 eggs
⅔ cup honey
1 quantity Royal Icing (page 121)

Preheat the oven to 350°F.

Sift the flour, baking powder, spices and pepper into a bowl. Add the grated lemon and orange zests. Beat in the eggs and honey, and knead the mixture into a stiff dough.

Roll out the dough on a lightly floured board and cut it into attractive shapes with cookie cutters. Transfer the shapes to greased baking sheets, and bake for 20 minutes.

Dilute the icing with about 2 tbsp water to make a pouring consistency. Transfer the cookies to wire racks and pour the icing over them in a thin glaze. The glaze should crack as it dries. Store in airtight tins with plenty of confectioners' sugar.

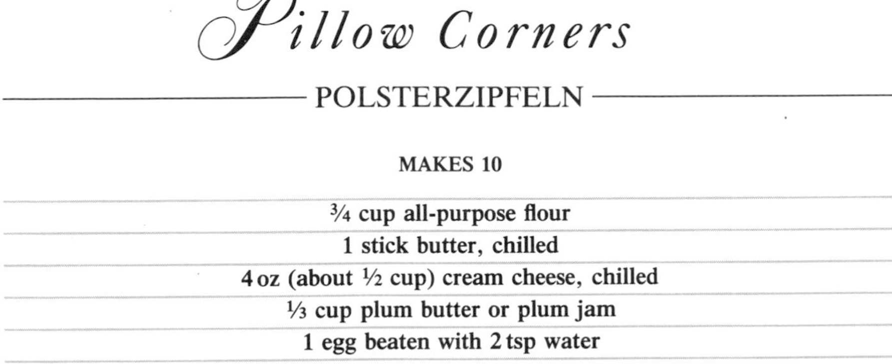

Pillow Corners

POLSTERZIPFELN

MAKES 10

¾ cup all-purpose flour
1 stick butter, chilled
4 oz (about ½ cup) cream cheese, chilled
⅓ cup plum butter or plum jam
1 egg beaten with 2 tsp water

Sift the flour on to a work surface. Cut the butter and cream cheese into small pieces and work them lightly into the flour, kneading with cool hands just until you have a firm dough. Wrap the dough and refrigerate for at least 2 hours or overnight.

Preheat the oven to 400°F. Roll out the dough into a rectangle about ⅛ inch thick. Cut it into 2 inch squares, using a ravioli cutter or sharp knife. Place 1 tsp plum butter or jam in the center of each square and fold over the squares into triangles, moistening the edges to seal them. Brush with the beaten egg.

Place on a greased baking sheet, and bake for 20 minutes or until golden brown.

Wood Shavings

HOBELSPÄNE

MAKES 10

5 eggs
1¼ cups granulated sugar
¾ cup all-purpose flour, sifted
¼ cup confectioners' sugar

Preheat the oven to 350°F.

Beat the eggs and granulated sugar together until thick and light. Beat in the flour. Spread this batter over a greased baking sheet.

Bake for 10 minutes. While still hot, quickly slice the cake into strips about 1 inch wide and 3 inches long and wind the strips around the handle of a wooden spoon. Cool on wire racks, and sprinkle with sifted confectioners' sugar when cold.

Tower Cakes

TÜRMCHEN

MAKES 30

6 eggs
¾ cup sugar
1⅔ cups all-purpose flour, sifted
4 tbsp butter, melted and cooled
1 quantity Vanilla Cream (page 124)
2 tsp Amaretto or Kirsch
2 tbsp strawberry jam, sieved
2 oz semisweet chocolate
⅓ cup cake or graham cracker crumbs
½ quantity Fondant Icing (page 121)
½ quantity Royal Icing (page 121), colored pink
½ quantity chocolate glaze for Little Indian Cakes (page 97)

Preheat the oven to 325°F. Line a jelly roll pan with nonstick parchment paper.

Beat the eggs and sugar in the top of a double boiler or a large bowl over simmering water until the mixture is thick. Remove from the heat and beat in the flour and butter. Spread the mixture ½ inch thick in the prepared pan.

Bake for 15 minutes; do not let the sponge mixture color. While it is still hot, cut out 30 rounds with a 1½ inch cutter. Cool the sponge rounds on wire racks.

Divide the vanilla cream into 3 portions. Add the liqueur to one part and the strawberry jam to the second part. Melt the chocolate in a bowl over boiling water and add it to the third part.

Top 10 of the sponge rounds with a mound of the liqueur cream. Top 10 rounds with jam cream, and the remaining rounds with chocolate cream. Sprinkle with the crumbs and refrigerate for 30 minutes.

Ice with fondant icing, pink-colored royal icing or chocolate glaze, depending on the flavor of the cream you have used for each cake.

Almond Rusks

MANDELBROT

This is a quick, modern recipe adapted from a traditional favorite. Instead of laboriously beating egg whites into stiff peaks the eggs are mixed in whole and baking powder is added to make the mixture rise.

MAKES ABOUT 30

3 eggs
¾ cup sugar
2½ cups all-purpose flour, sifted
1 tsp baking powder
1½ sticks (6 oz) butter, melted
1 tsp almond extract
¾ cup coarsely chopped blanched almonds
1 tbsp ground cinnamon mixed with 6 tbsp sugar

Preheat the oven to 350°F.

Beat the eggs and sugar together until the mixture is light and fluffy. Beat in the flour, baking powder, melted butter, almond extract and almonds. Mix well; the dough should be very stiff.

Divide the dough into three portions and shape each into a sausage shape about 3 inches in diameter. Place on a greased and floured baking sheet, and bake for 30 minutes or until lightly browned.

Remove from the oven and slice the sausages at an angle into ½ inch thick slices. Grease the baking sheet again and arrange the slices, cut sides up, on the sheet (you may need an extra baking sheet). Sprinkle them with the cinnamon-and-sugar mixture. Return to the oven and bake for another 10 minutes. Cool on wire racks. They will keep very well in an airtight tin.

Little Indian Cakes

INDIANERKRAPFEN

These cakes are not difficult to make, but need a little care in assembling. Make sure to leave a thick enough shell when removing the centers, or the filling will melt when the glaze is poured over the cakes. Refrigerate the cream as described at each stage so that it will be thick enough to retain its shape. Eat these on the same day they are made.

MAKES 12

¼ cup all-purpose flour	***Chocolate glaze***
¼ cup cornstarch	**4 oz semisweet chocolate**
4 eggs, separated	**⅔ cup heavy cream**
6 tbsp vanilla sugar	**1 cup sugar**
Filling	**¼ cup water**
1½ cups heavy cream	**2 tbsp light corn syrup**
1 tbsp vanilla sugar	**1 egg, lightly beaten**
	1 tsp vanilla extract

Preheat the oven to 400°F.

Butter and flour two 6 cup muffin tins.

Sift the flour and cornstarch into a bowl. In another bowl, whisk the egg yolks with the vanilla sugar until the mixture is light and fluffy. Beat the egg whites into stiff peaks and fold them into the egg yolk mixture. Sprinkle with the flour mixture and fold together until the mixture is smooth.

Pour the mixture into the tins so that it comes two-thirds of the way up the cups. Bake for 12 minutes or until lightly browned. Remove the tins from the oven and run a knife around the inside of each cup to loosen the cake. Unmold the cakes on to wire racks to cool.

To make the filling, whip the cream until it starts to thicken, then add the vanilla sugar and whip until the cream holds its shape. Refrigerate until required.

Use a very sharp knife to cut out the center of each cake, leaving a ¼ inch thick ring around the sides and bottom of each cake. (The centers can be ground and used as cake crumbs in another recipe.) Fill each cake shell with the cream and refrigerate for at least 1 hour.

To make the chocolate glaze, combine the chocolate, cream, sugar, water and corn syrup in a heavy-based saucepan. Stir the mixture over low heat until the chocolate has melted and the sugar dissolved, then increase the heat and cook for another 5 minutes without stirring.

Remove the pan from the heat and cool for 5 minutes. Beat 1 tbsp of the glaze into the egg, then beat this mixture into the rest of the glaze. Add the vanilla extract.

Arrange the cakes, with the cream filling downward, on wire racks. Pour the glaze over them and leave it to set for 10 minutes, before refrigerating. Serve when cold.

Desserts

Salzburg Soufflé

SALZBURGER NOCKERLN

Nockerln are usually little pasta shapes to put into soup, so the German name for this recipe is very misleading. Although spoonbread is usually thought to be of Native American origin, it is suspiciously similar to the Salzburg Soufflé and would have been very hard to make without sophisticated equipment, so I think this is the original spoonbread.

SERVES 4–6

6 tbsp butter, softened
8 eggs, separated
3 tbsp all-purpose flour, sifted
½ cup vanilla sugar
¼ cup hot milk
¼ cup confectioners' sugar

Butter a 1½ quart glass baking dish or 6 individual 4 inch diameter soufflé dishes.

Preheat the oven to 350°F.

Cream the butter with the egg yolks. Beat in the flour and continue beating until the mixture is light and fluffy. Beat the egg whites into stiff peaks, then gradually beat in the vanilla sugar; the mixture should be very stiff. Fold the egg white mixture into the egg yolk mixture.

Pour the hot milk into the prepared baking dish (or dishes). Pour the egg mixture on top of it, and bake for 15 minutes or until the top is lightly browned. Turn off the oven and leave the pudding in it for another 30 minutes to cool gradually. It will rise as it cooks, but sink and crack on cooling. This is normal, so don't worry that something has gone wrong. Sprinkle generously with sifted confectioners' sugar and serve while still warm.

Semolina Cake With Wine Sauce

GRIESSTORTE MIT WEINSCHAUM

This cake shows Turkish influence in its use of semolina and sauce, so that it more closely resembles Middle Eastern pâtisserie than a European recipe. The wine in the sauce is, however, a distinctly Austrian touch.

SERVES 10

6 eggs, separated	***Wine sauce***
1 cup granulated sugar	**4 egg yolks**
grated zest and juice of 1 lemon	**6 tbsp sugar**
¾ cup ground almonds	**1¼ cups sweet red or white wine**
1 cup semolina flour or farina	**1 strip of lemon zest**
2 tbsp vanilla sugar	

Preheat the oven to 350°F. Butter and flour an 8 inch square cake pan.

Beat the egg yolks with the granulated sugar until thick and pale. Add the lemon zest and juice, ground almonds, semolina flour and vanilla sugar. Beat the egg whites into stiff peaks and fold them into the mixture. Turn into the prepared pan and bake for 40 minutes.

Meanwhile, prepare the wine sauce. In the top of a double boiler or large bowl, combine the egg yolks, sugar and wine, and add the lemon zest. Stir with a wooden spoon over hot water until the mixture is thick enough to coat the spoon. Discard the lemon zest.

Serve the cake warm. Pour some hot wine sauce over it and serve the rest on the side.

Moor In A Shirt

MOHR IM HEMD

This cooked chocolate pudding is so-called because of the contrast between the white cream and the dark chocolate. It makes an elegant dinner-party dessert, but should be prepared a day ahead.

SERVES 6

4 tbsp butter, softened	***Icing***
5 eggs, separated	**⅔ cup sugar**
½ cup granulated sugar	**⅓ cup water**
3 oz semisweet chocolate, grated	**4 egg whites**
1½ cups ground almonds	**1 tbsp rum**
½ cup heavy cream	
3 tbsp confectioners' sugar, sifted	
1 tbsp rum	
crystallized violets, to decorate (optional)	

Grease a round deep steaming mold and sprinkle it evenly with granulated sugar, shaking out the excess.

Beat the butter until it is fluffy, then beat in the egg yolks, one at a time. Beat in the granulated sugar, chocolate and almonds. Beat the egg whites until stiff and fold them into the mixture.

Spoon into the prepared mold. Cover the mold with greased foil and tie on securely. Stand it in a saucepan of hot water, so the water comes two-thirds of the way up the sides, and cover the pan. Put it over low heat and simmer for 1 hour. Unmold it immediately on to a serving dish.

To make the icing, dissolve the sugar in the water, then boil for 15 minutes, or to the large thread stage. Meanwhile, beat the egg whites until stiff. Pour the hot syrup slowly into the egg whites, beating continuously, then beat in the rum as the mixture thickens. Beat until quite stiff.

Pour the icing over the pudding, smoothing it down with a palette knife. Leave to cool, then refrigerate.

Just before serving, whip the cream with the confectioners' sugar and rum and use to decorate the pudding, with crystallized violets if liked.

Illustrated on pages 102–103

Moor In A Shirt

Emperor's Omelette

KAISERSCHMARRN

This sweet omelette is often served with stewed plums, cooked on the previous day in a little water with sugar, cinnamon and cloves.

SERVES 6

4 eggs, separated
3 tbsp granulated sugar
1 tbsp vanilla sugar
2 cups milk
¾ cup all-purpose flour
scant ½ cup golden raisins, soaked in 3 tbsp dark rum overnight
4 tbsp butter
⅓ cup confectioners' sugar
plum butter or stewed plums, to serve

Beat the egg yolks, granulated sugar and vanilla sugar until the mixture is foaming and pale yellow. Stir in the milk and gradually beat in the sifted flour. Continue to beat until the mixture is smooth.

Drain the raisins and pat them dry on paper towels. Stir them into the mixture. Beat the egg whites into stiff peaks and fold them into the egg yolk mixture.

Heat an 8 inch omelette pan over low heat and melt 1 tbsp of the butter in it, swirling around to coat it evenly. Pour in half the egg mixture and cook over low heat for 3 minutes, or until the omelette is puffy and can be seen to be lightly browned underneath when the edge is lifted with a metal spatula. Slide the omelette on to a plate. Add another 1 tbsp butter to the pan and melt it. Flip the omelette back into the pan, uncooked side down, and cook for another 3 minutes. Transfer to a warmed plate, and use 2 forks to pull the omelette into 6 pieces. Keep hot.

Repeat the process with the rest of the butter and egg mixture, pulling the omelette into portions when it is cooked. Sprinkle with the sifted confectioners' sugar, and serve hot with plum butter or stewed plums.

Austrian Bread Pudding

SCHEITERHAUFEN

This prince of bread puddings is probably the prototype of the alcohol-rich bread pudding so popular in New Orleans which, like all American ports, had a sizeable German-speaking population in the last century. In New Orleans, bourbon whiskey replaces the rum.

SERVES 6

2 tbsp golden raisins
2 tbsp raisins
6 tbsp dark rum
little all-purpose flour
6 slices day-old white bread, crusts removed
2 tbsp butter, softened
4 apples (about 1 lb), peeled, cored and sliced
1 tsp ground cinnamon
½ tsp grated nutmeg
½ tsp ground allspice
½ tsp ground cloves
4 egg yolks, lightly beaten
1 cup milk
1 cup light cream
2 tbsp sugar
1 quantity warm Vanilla Cream (page 124), flavored with rum, to serve

Soak the raisins in the rum overnight. Drain, reserving the rum, dry on paper towels and toss in flour. Preheat the oven to 350°F.

Butter the bread and cut it into fingers. Arrange a layer of the bread, buttered side up, in an 8 inch square baking dish and cover with a layer of apples. Sprinkle the apples with a layer of raisins. Cover with another bread layer and cover the bread with more apples and raisins. Continue until all the ingredients have been used up, finishing with a layer of bread.

Whisk the spices into the egg yolks, and beat in the milk, cream and sugar. Pour this liquid over the pudding and sprinkle the surface with the reserved rum.

Bake for 30 minutes or until the top is browned and the liquid set. Serve warm with vanilla cream.

Malakoff Charlotte

MALAKOFFTORTE

Despite strenuous efforts, I have been unable to discover why this rich charlotte-type pudding is named after General Aimable Jean-Jacques Pélissier, Duke of Malakoff (1794–1864), since he had no connection with Austria, though he did fight the Turks in the Crimean War. Yet this pudding is far more popular in Austria than it is in France. Malakoff has had several streets named after him there, as well as a suburb of Paris, but no pudding.

SERVES 10–12

Ladyfinger cookies	*Almond filling*
3 eggs, separated	6 tbsp butter, softened
½ cup + 2 tbsp sugar	4 egg yolks
½ cup + 2 tbsp all-purpose flour, sifted	1 cup sugar
pinch of salt	1¾ cups ground almonds
	1 tsp almond or bitter almond extract
	2 cups heavy cream

Preheat the oven to 300°F. Line 3 baking sheets with nonstick parchment paper.

To make the cookies, beat the egg yolks with ½ cup of the sugar until light and fluffy. Fold in the flour. Beat the egg whites with the salt into stiff peaks. Gently fold the egg whites into the egg yolk.

Fit a plain ½ inch diameter tube in a pastry bag. Put the mixture into the pastry bag and pipe 4 inch fingerlike strips onto the baking paper, leaving about 1 inch between each finger. Sprinkle the fingers with the remaining 2 tbsp sugar and bake for 15–18 minutes or until very lightly browned. Leave the ladyfingers to cool completely before removing them from the paper. Store in an airtight tin with plenty of confectioners' sugar for at least 48 hours before using.

To make the almond filling, beat the butter and egg yolks with all but 1 tbsp of the sugar, the almonds, almond extract and half the cream.

Line a 7 inch charlotte mold or springform pan with nonstick parchment paper, cut to fit the bottom and inside of the mold or pan.

Arrange a ring of ladyfingers standing upright around the sides of the mold or pan and over the bottom, and pour half the filling over them. Cover with another layer of ladyfingers and pour the rest of the almond filling over them. Top with the remaining ladyfingers. Put the base of a cake pan on top of the mixture and put weights such as cans of food on top. Refrigerate overnight.

When ready to serve, unmold the charlotte. Whip the rest of the cream with the reserved tablespoon of sugar and spread some over the top. Put the rest into a pastry bag fitted with a star tube and pipe cream decorations over the cake. Tie a ribbon around the cake before serving, and if liked decorate with sugared almonds and silver candy balls.

Confectionery

Parisian Bars

PARISERSTANGEL

MAKES ABOUT 40

1⅓ cups ground hazelnuts (filberts)
½ cup sugar
1 egg white, lightly beaten
1 tsp apricot jam, sieved
1 quantity Royal Icing (page 121)

Cover a baking sheet with rice paper.

Combine the hazelnuts, sugar, egg white and jam into a dough. Roll out the dough into a rectangle ¼ inch thick and slice it into 2 × 4 inch strips. Lay the strips on the rice paper and ice them with the royal icing. Leave the icing to dry for 10 minutes.

Preheat the oven to 300°F. Slice the strips in half lengthwise, to make narrow bars. Bake for 15 minutes. Trim away excess rice paper and cool on wire racks.

Stuffed Figs

GEFÜLLTE FEIGEN

MAKES 10

With choc. truffle mixture

10 large dried figs
4 oz semisweet chocolate
1 stick butter
¼ cup cocoa powder

Put the figs into a saucepan and add water to cover. Bring to a boil and simmer for 10 minutes. Rinse the figs in cold water and pat them dry with paper towels.

Scoop out the centers of the figs, and discard. Melt the chocolate in a small bowl or top of a double boiler over simmering water. When melted, add the butter and stir until smooth. Cool the mixture and refrigerate it until firm.

Stuff the figs with the chocolate mixture. Roll them in cocoa and put in paper candy (bonbon) cases.

Dominoes

DOMINOSTEINE

MAKES ABOUT 20

2⅓ cups ground hazelnuts (filberts)
1 cup granulated sugar
3 oz semisweet chocolate, grated
about 2 egg whites
about ⅓ cup confectioners' sugar
½ quantity Royal Icing (page 121)
¼ quantity Chocolate Icing (page 120)

Combine the hazelnuts, sugar and chocolate in a bowl and beat in enough egg white to make a firm paste. Sprinkle a work surface and a rolling pin with sifted confectioners' sugar and roll out the mixture into a rectangle about ¼ inch thick. Slice the mixture into bars about 1 × 2 inches. Leave them to dry overnight.

The next day, ice the bars with the royal icing. Put the chocolate icing into a pastry bag fitted with a small plain tube and pipe dividing lines and domino dots on the bars.

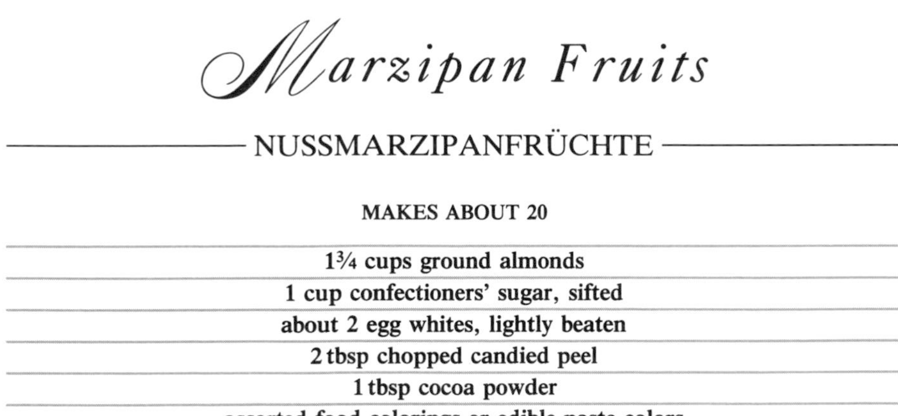

Marzipan Fruits

NUSSMARZIPANFRÜCHTE

MAKES ABOUT 20

1¾ cups ground almonds
1 cup confectioners' sugar, sifted
about 2 egg whites, lightly beaten
2 tbsp chopped candied peel
1 tbsp cocoa powder
assorted food colorings or edible paste colors

Mix the ground nuts with the confectioners' sugar and moisten with enough egg white to make a firm paste. Take a few pieces of candied peel and wrap paste around it. Shape into potatoes, carrots, mushrooms, apples, pears and strawberries. Dip the "potatoes" in cocoa. Use a soft paintbrush to paint the other fruits with appropriate colorings. Dry on wire racks covered with nonstick parchment paper.

Serve in paper candy (bonbon) cases.

Illustrated on page 110

Marzipan Fruits & Cinnamon Stars

Fruit Sausage

FRÜCHTENWURST

MAKES ABOUT 20 SLICES

½ lb pitted prunes (about 1½ cups)
½ lb pitted dried apricots (about 1½ cups)
½ lb pitted dried dates (about 1½ cups)
½ lb dried figs (about 1½ cups)
6 tbsp confectioners' sugar
3 tbsp honey
1 cup finely chopped walnuts

Chop the dried fruits coarsely and grind them together in a food processor. Add the sifted confectioners' sugar, honey and nuts.

Turn out the fruit mixture on to a work surface sprinkled with more confectioners' sugar. Knead and form into a sausage shape. Leave it to dry out at room temperature overnight. Store in an airtight tin.

When ready to serve, cut into ½ inch diagonal slices.

Chocolate Hazelnut Candies

SCHOKOLADENHASELNUSSBONBONS

MAKES ABOUT 40

2 heaping cups shelled hazelnuts (filberts)
2 tbsp water
1½ cups granulated sugar
1 quantity Fondant Icing (page 121)
sifted confectioners' sugar
1 quantity Chocolate Icing (page 120)

Put the hazelnuts into a dry nonstick skillet and toast, stirring occasionally, over low heat until they begin to give out their aroma. Tip the nuts on to a dish towel and rub to remove the skins.

Grind the nuts in a food processor with the water and granulated sugar. Add the fondant icing and knead on a work surface dusted with confectioners' sugar to make a paste.

Roll out the paste until it is ½ inch thick. Use very small cutters or a sharp knife to cut it into attractive shapes. Dip them in the chocolate icing. Dry them on wire racks covered with nonstick parchment paper.
Illustrated on page 115

Cinnamon Stars

ZIMTSTERNE

MAKES ABOUT 30

1 cup + 2 tbsp granulated sugar	***Icing***
1 tsp ground cinnamon	**1 cup confectioners' sugar, sifted**
2 cups ground almonds	**2 tsp lemon juice**
about ½ egg white	
2 tbsp water	
sifted confectioners' sugar	

Preheat the oven to its lowest setting. Line a baking sheet with nonstick parchment paper, and sprinkle the baking paper with sifted confectioners' sugar.

Mix together the granulated sugar, cinnamon and ground almonds. Make a well in the center and add the egg white and water. Knead into a firm dough; if the mixture is too dry to cohere, add a little more egg white.

Sprinkle a rolling pin with confectioners' sugar and roll out the mixture on a work surface dusted with more confectioners' sugar until it is ¼ inch thick. Cut it into stars with a small star-shaped cookie cutter.

Arrange the stars on the baking sheet and dry them out in the oven for 20 minutes. Increase the oven heat to 300°F and bake for 30 minutes longer. Cool on wire racks.

Mix the confectioners' sugar with the lemon juice and spread this icing over the stars. If liked, decorate with colored or confetti sugar. Leave to dry. Store in airtight tins with plenty of confectioners' sugar.

Illustrated on page 110

Mozart Chocolate Truffles & Chocolate Hazelnut Candies

Quince Paste Candies

QUITTENBROT

These are unmistakably of oriental origin, via the Turks. The Arabs brought quinces from China during the Middle Ages, and they still feature extensively in Middle Eastern cooking. Quinces are in season in late fall. They are like very tough, indigestible apples and can only be eaten cooked. When cooked they turn a pleasing pink color and are very aromatic.

MAKES ABOUT 2 lb

4½ lb quinces, scraped, quartered and cored
2 whole cloves
3 allspice berries
1 cinnamon stick
about 2½ lb (5 cups) + 6 tbsp sugar
3 tbsp Kirsch

Put the quinces into a large pan and add cold water to cover. Tie the cloves, allspice and cinnamon in a piece of cheesecloth or other porous cloth and put it in the water. Bring slowly to a boil, cover the pan and simmer gently for 45 minutes. Remove from the heat and let stand, covered, overnight.

The next day, drain the quinces, discarding the bag of spices (the cooking water can be used as a cold drink or for stewing other fruit). Sieve the quinces or purée them in a food processor and then sieve to remove any seeds and fibers. Measure the purée and combine it with the same quantity of sugar.

Put the sweetened purée into a heavy-based pan. Cook, stirring constantly, over low heat until the mixture comes away from the sides of the pan. Remove from the heat and add the Kirsch.

Rinse two 8 × 10 inch jelly roll pans with water, and spread out the quince mixture in the pans, smoothing it flat with a palette knife. Put them into an oven on its lowest setting (there is no need to preheat it) or in a gas oven with a pilot light. Leave to dry for as long as possible, but at least 5 hours.

Remove from the oven and cut into ½ inch squares. Put 6 tbsp sugar into a bowl, and dip the squares in the sugar to coat them thoroughly. Put them into paper candy (bonbon) cases for serving.

Mozart Chocolate Truffles

MOZARTKUGELN

The famous Mozartkugeln are a specialty of Salzburg, Mozart's home town. Whether he ate them is not recorded, but he certainly did have a sweet tooth.

MAKES 24

4 tbsp butter, softened
2 egg yolks
¼ cup confectioners' sugar
1 cup cocoa powder
6 oz semisweet chocolate, grated
6 oz milk chocolate

Cover a baking sheet with wax or nonstick parchment paper. Beat the butter and egg yolks with the sifted confectioners' sugar until light and creamy. Add the cocoa and grated chocolate. Knead the mixture thoroughly, then shape it into balls about ½ inch in diameter. Arrange the balls on the baking sheet and refrigerate for 30 minutes.

Melt the milk chocolate in a bowl over simmering water. Remove the truffle balls on their baking sheet from the refrigerator. Insert a toothpick into each ball and dip it in the melted milk chocolate, coating it evenly. Twirl it in the air for a few moments to cool it, then place it on the baking sheet and gently remove the toothpick, smearing over the hole it has left with your finger. When all the balls have been dipped, return them to the refrigerator to chill for at least 30 minutes.

Wrap each ball in cellophane or a sheet of thin foil, or present in paper candy (bonbon) cases.
Illustrated on page 114

Basic Recipes

Shortcake Dough

MÜRBETEIG

MAKES ABOUT 1½ lb

2 sticks (8 oz) butter
2 cups all-purpose flour, sifted
6 tbsp sugar
⅛ tsp salt
1 egg yolk
¼ cup milk

Work the butter into the flour using knives, a pastry cutter or a food processor until the mixture resembles bread crumbs. Add the other ingredients and work the mixture into a smooth dough. Wrap and leave it in a cool place such as the refrigerator, for at least 1 hour before using.

Basic Sponge Cake

SANDTORTE

SERVES 8–10

1½ sticks (6 oz) butter, softened
4 eggs, separated
¾ cup sugar
1 tsp vanilla extract
1 cup all-purpose flour, sifted
1 tsp baking powder

Preheat the oven to 350°F. Grease and flour a deep 8 inch cake pan or 2 layer cake pans, shaking out the excess flour.

Cream the butter with the egg yolks and sugar until light and fluffy. Add the vanilla extract. Sift the flour and baking powder into the bowl and beat into the creamed mixture. Beat the egg whites into stiff peaks and fold them into the mixture.

Turn the mixture into the pan or pans. Bake for 40 minutes if using one cake pan, 25 minutes for 2 pans. Place the pan on a wire rack to cool for 5 minutes, then unmold to cool.

Yeast Puff Dough

GERMBUTTERTEIG

This is the dough used to make the so-called "Danish" pastry, which the French call viennoiserie and the Danish call wienerbrød. It can be cut into traditional Danish pastry shapes (coxcombs, pockets, etc.) and filled and iced in that way, or shaped into croissants, filled or unfilled. Making the dough is a slow process, because it has to rest so often. Allow at least 36 hours between starting the dough and baking the finished product; the 1 hour resting time between rollings is a minimum, and can be increased to overnight if convenient.

MAKES 1½ lb

1 oz compressed yeast, or 2 packages active dry yeast
about ½ cup milk, at blood heat
1⅔ cups all-purpose flour
¼ tsp salt
1 tbsp sugar
1 egg yolk
2 sticks (8 oz) butter

Cream the compressed yeast with the milk, or stir dried yeast into the milk until dissolved, and leave in a warm place until foaming, about 20 minutes.

Sift the flour and salt into the bowl of a heavy-duty (countertop) electric mixer. Make a well in the center and pour the yeast mixture into it. Add the sugar and egg yolk. Cut 4 tbsp of the butter into pieces and add them to the liquid. Gradually incorporate the flour into the liquid mixture until you obtain a soft, sticky dough. Work the dough with the dough hook until it is smooth and elastic, about 5 minutes. Put it into a greased bowl, cover and leave to rise in a warm place until doubled in bulk, about 2 hours.

Punch down the dough, cover it again and leave it to rise again, either at room temperature for 1 hour or in the refrigerator overnight.

Soften the rest of the butter. On a lightly floured work surface, roll out the dough with a floured rolling pin into a rectangle about ½ inch thick and twice as long as it is wide. Smear two-thirds of the rectangle with the rest of the butter, leaving an unbuttered margin around the edges of the dough of ½ inch, so the butter will not escape when the dough is folded. Fold the unbuttered third of the dough over half the buttered section, then fold the remaining buttered section over the top of the other two; there will be three layers of dough with butter between each. Press the edges of the dough with the rolling pin to seal them. Turn the dough a quarter-turn and roll it out lightly, trying to avoid pressing the butter out of it. Continue rolling until the dough is once again twice as long as it is wide. Fold it in three again as before. Wrap the dough and chill for 1 hour.

Roll out the dough again and fold it in three as before. Wrap it and chill for another hour.

Repeat the process once more, resting the dough for 1 hour between rollings. It is now ready for use.

Boiled Icing

GEKOCHTEGLAZUR

This rich and very delicious icing must be used at once or it will dry out and become unusable. It is best made without coloring, because it will not blend in smoothly enough.

TO ICE ONE 10 inch CAKE

1 cup granulated sugar
½ cup water
2 cups confectioners' sugar, sifted
1 tbsp lemon juice or colorless liqueur

Put the granulated sugar and water into a heavy-based saucepan. Bring to a boil over medium heat, brushing away any crystals that form on the sides of the pan using a pastry brush dipped in water. Boil the syrup, without stirring, for about 10 minutes or until it reaches the soft ball stage (page 13).

Remove the pan from the heat and gradually beat in the confectioners' sugar. Beat in the lemon juice or liqueur. Coat the cake as soon as the icing cools to lukewarm.

Chocolate Icing

SCHOKOLADENGLAZUR

TO ICE ONE 8 inch CAKE

2 cups sugar
½ cup water
5 oz semisweet chocolate
1 tbsp butter

Put the sugar and water into a heavy-based saucepan. Bring to a boil over medium heat, brushing away any crystals that form on the sides of the pan using a pastry brush dipped in water. Boil the syrup, without stirring, for about 10 minutes or until it reaches the large thread stage (page 13).

Meanwhile put the chocolate in a bowl or the top of a double boiler and melt it over simmering water. Add the butter, and stir until smooth.

Gradually pour the hot syrup over the chocolate mixture, stirring constantly with a metal spoon until the icing is thick enough to coat the back of the spoon.

For ***Coffee Icing***, replace the water with strong black coffee.

For ***Spicy Icing*** (very good with plain sponge cakes and poppyseed cake), add 1 tsp each of apple pie spice and cinnamon and a pinch of ground cloves.

Royal Icing

EIWEISSGLAZUR

TO ICE ONE 10 inch CAKE

1 egg white
1¾ cups confectioners' sugar, sifted
1–2 tbsp lemon, orange or pineapple juice or liqueur

Beat the egg white into the confectioners' sugar until the mixture is smooth. Beat in enough fruit juice or liqueur to give the icing a spreading consistency. Use immediately.

For ***Glacé Icing***, thin the icing by gradually adding water until it has a runny consistency. It is then suitable for icing cookies and dark-colored cakes such as Poppyseed Sponge Cake (page 21).

For ***Rum Punch Icing***, use rum for the flavoring and color the icing pink with 2–3 drops of food coloring.

Fondant Icing

FONDANTGLAZUR

TO ICE ONE 10 inch CAKE

2 cups sugar
⅔ cup water
2 tbsp light corn syrup
about ¼ cup cornstarch

Sprinkle a marble slab or large dish with water. Put all the ingredients except the cornstarch into a heavy-based saucepan. Bring to a boil over medium heat, brushing away any crystals that form on the sides of the pan using a pastry brush dipped in water. Boil the syrup, without stirring, for about 10 minutes or until it reaches the soft ball stage.

Pour the syrup quickly over the prepared slab or dish and work by folding the sides to the center, using a wet metal scraper or palette knife, until the mixture is no longer transparent and has become white and creamy. When it becomes completely opaque and crumbly, dust your hands with cornstarch and knead the mixture into the consistency of a firm dough. At this stage, it can be wrapped and refrigerated. It will keep almost indefinitely.

When ready to use it, knead in 2 tbsp of any of the icing flavorings given in other recipes. As soon as the icing has the consistency of a firm dough again, dust a work surface and rolling pin with cornstarch and roll out the icing into a sheet about ¼ inch thick. Wrap it loosely around the rolling pin and drape it over the cake to be iced. Trim off any surplus with a sharp knife and store it again for future use.

Strudel Fillings

STRUDELFÜLLUNGEN

All of these fillings are sufficient to fill the strudel for which the recipe is given on page 42. They can also be used to fill any other kind of cake, and are especially suitable to fill the jelly roll-type cakes, such as Chocolate-Filled Yeast Roll (page 71) and Austrian Jam Roll (page 44). Leftover filling can be stored in containers and refrigerated or frozen until required.

Apple Filling
APFELFÜLLUNG

MAKES 2 lb

- **4 tbsp butter**
- **1½ cups cake crumbs**
- **3 lb apples, peeled, cored and sliced**
- **grated zest and juice of 1 lemon**
- **½ cup sugar**
- **3 tbsp golden raisins**

Melt the butter in a skillet and add the crumbs, stirring to coat them well with butter. Sprinkle the strudel or other dough with the buttered crumbs, then arrange the apples over them. Sprinkle with the lemon juice, then add the lemon zest, sugar and raisins. Roll up and bake as directed.

Cherry Filling
KIRSCHFÜLLUNG

MAKES 2 lb

- **4 tbsp butter**
- **1½ cups cake crumbs**
- **3 lb cherries, pitted**
- **grated zest and juice of 1 lemon**
- **½ cup sugar**
- **2 tbsp cherry brandy or Kirsch**

Melt the butter in a skillet and add the crumbs, stirring to coat them well with butter. Sprinkle the strudel or other dough with the buttered crumbs, then arrange the cherries over them. Sprinkle with the lemon juice, then add the lemon zest, sugar and liqueur. Roll up and bake as directed.

Sour Cream Filling
RAHMFÜLLUNG

Thick plain yogurt can be substituted for the sour cream. Cakes and strudels filled with sour cream should be lavishly sprinkled with sugar and served with Vanilla Cream (page 124).

MAKES 1½ lb

5 tbsp butter, softened
6 tbsp sugar
4 eggs, separated
¼ cup sour cream
1 lb (about 2 cups) medium- or low-fat cream cheese
½ tsp grated lemon zest
2 tbsp golden raisins

Beat the butter, sugar and egg yolks together. Beat in the sour cream, then the cheese and lemon zest. Beat the egg whites into stiff peaks and fold them into the mixture. Spread the mixture over the dough and sprinkle with the raisins before rolling.

Poppyseed Filling
MOHNFÜLLUNG

MAKES 1 lb

2 cups poppyseeds
1½ cups milk
1 stick butter, softened
3 tbsp clear honey
grated zest of 1 lemon
1 tsp vanilla extract
1 tsp ground cinnamon
1 tbsp golden raisins, chopped
2 tbsp chopped mixed candied peel

Grind the poppyseeds in a spice grinder or coffee grinder or with a pestle and mortar. Put them into a bowl and pour the milk over them. Leave at room temperature to soak for at least 2 hours.

Combine the rest of the ingredients in a saucepan and cook, stirring, over low heat for 3 minutes. Add the poppyseed mixture, and cook, stirring, until thickened. Spread on the dough, roll up and bake as directed.

Vanilla Cream

VANILLECREME

This mixture doubles as a dessert sauce and as a cake filling. As a sauce, it is an especially good partner to strudels of all kinds. As a cake filling it makes a striking color contrast in a chocolate cake. It can be made well in advance.

MAKES 1½ cups

¾ cup light cream
¾ cup sugar
4 egg yolks
1–3 tsp cornstarch
2 inch piece vanilla bean
1½ sticks (6 oz) butter, softened

Combine the cream, sugar, egg yolks and 1 tsp cornstarch in the top of a double boiler. If the mixture is to be used as a cake filling, add the extra cornstarch. Slit the vanilla bean on one side so the seeds can be released. Discard them and add the bean to the mixture. Stir well over gently boiling water until the mixture is thick, then remove and discard the vanilla bean. Serve hot or cold as a sauce.

If the mixture is to be used as a cake filling, beat the butter until it is light and fluffy, then stir it into the slightly cooled mixture. Cool to room temperature, then refrigerate until required.

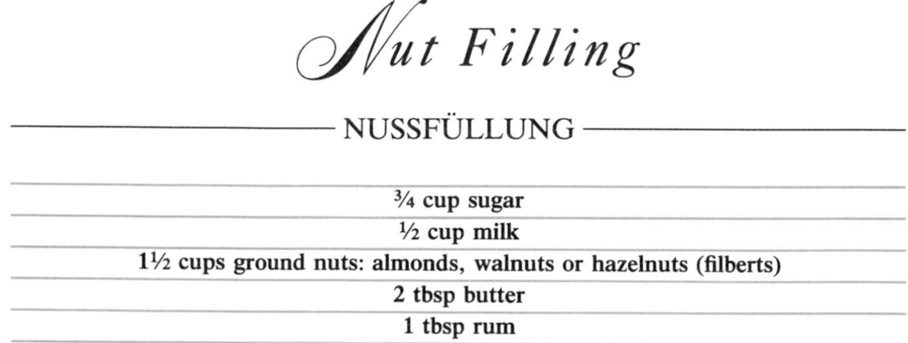

Nut Filling

NUSSFÜLLUNG

¾ cup sugar
½ cup milk
1½ cups ground nuts: almonds, walnuts or hazelnuts (filberts)
2 tbsp butter
1 tbsp rum

Combine the sugar with the milk in a saucepan. Stir well over a gentle heat until the sugar dissolves, then bring to a boil, stirring constantly. Remove from the heat and stir in the rest of the ingredients. Leave to cool before using.

Coffee Praline Cream

GRILLAGECREME

This is a very popular filling and icing for cakes made with ground nuts. If you cannot find hazelnuts that have been skinned, they are easily peeled by toasting them in a dry skillet, then rubbing them in a dish towel until the skins fall off. Other kinds of nuts, such as almonds, cashews and even peanuts, can also be used. Praline has all sorts of other uses – as a covering for the side of a cake, for instance, as a decoration instead of chocolate sprinkles or confetti sugar, and if left whole, simply as a delicious candy.

MAKES 1¼ lb (enough for filling and icing one 10 inch cake)

1 cup sugar
¾ cup shelled peeled hazelnuts (filberts)
2 sticks (8 oz) butter
2 tsp instant coffee powder

Oil a marble slab or baking sheet. If using a baking sheet, chill it first in the refrigerator for 30 minutes. Put ¾ cup of the sugar and the hazelnuts into a heavy-based saucepan. Cook over very low heat, stirring constantly with a wooden spoon or spatula, to melt and crystallize the sugar and coat the nuts. When the sugar syrup turns yellow, quickly pour the mixture on to the marble slab or baking sheet and spread it out with the spoon or spatula.

Leave the nut mixture to cool completely and set, then put it into a plastic bag and crush it with a rolling pin until it is evenly crumbled. The praline can also be ground in a food processor.

Beat the butter until it is light and fluffy. Add the rest of the sugar, the praline and the coffee. When the mixture is well combined, refrigerate it until required.

Two cups heavy cream can be whipped and substituted for the butter if the praline cream is to be used at once. This would also make a delicious dessert sauce.

For ***Chocolate Praline Cream***, replace the coffee with 1 tbsp cocoa powder.

Index

Note Numbers in italics refer to illustrations

Cookies
Date Bars - 73
Corsicans - 73
Chestnut squares 77
cream cheese filled bars 79
crescents - 84
mandelbrot
Parisian Bars 108

Danish (yeast Puff Dough)
Crown Cake (pastry - 54
Danish pastry 119
cheese Danish 70

Rehrücken molds (Balmoral tins), springform tins and gold and silver sweet boxes supplied by Covent Garden Kitchen Supplies, 3 North Row, The Market, Covent Garden, London WC2; Victorian etched glass *c* 1860, brilliant cut and acid etched Victorian glass *c* 1890 and Art Nouveau stained glass window *c* 1910 supplied by Townsends, 36 New End Square, Hampstead, London NW3

Tortes

Chestnut Torte 16
Dobos torte 22
* Rehrucken (graham cracker crumbs) 24
Sachertorte - 25
Best Choc. almond cake 28
* Nut torte - Coffee praline cream 37
*** Rum Punch cake 38
Chocolate hazelnut cake 46
Choc. Wafer cake (Oblaten wafers) 52

misc:

Coffee Praline Cream 125

Coffee Cakes etc

B.P. marble gugelhupf 48
Baking Powder Gugelhupf 53
Nut gugelhupf (yeast) 58
Crumb cake (Streusel) (yeast) 65
Sour Cream Muffins - 81
Emperor's pancake 104

Pastries, Tarts

* Linzertorte P. 14
** Strawberry Tart 17 (picture P. 19)
** Swedish apple tart (meringue topping) 20
* Napoleons with ice cream 76

Streudel fillings 122-23

Desserts

Salzburg Nockerln 98
Semolina cake 100
Moor in a Shirt (gr. almonds) - 101
Austrian Bread pudding with apples 105
Charlotte Malakoff (almond filling) 106

Confectionary

XXX Stuffed figs 108
Dominos - 109
** Marzipan - 109
Picture 110
** Fruit sausage 112
Cinnamon stars 113
XXXX Quince paste candies 116
XXX Mozart balls 117